TEACHER PROFESSIONALISM AND THE CHALLENGE OF CHANGE

EDITED BY JIM GRAHAM

UNIVERSITY OF EAST LONDON
STUDIES IN EDUCATION NUMBER 1

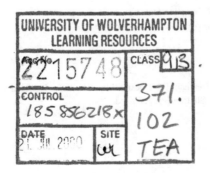

Trentham Books

First published in 1999 by Trentham Books Limited

Trentham Books Limited
Westview House
734 London Road
Oakhill
Stoke on Trent
Staffordshire
England ST4 5NP

British Cataloguing in Publication Data
A catalogue record for this book is available from the
British Library
ISBN 1 85856 218 X

Designed and typeset by Trentham Print Design Ltd., Chester and printed in
Great Britain by Bemrose Shafron (Printers) Ltd.

CONTENTS

PREFACE

JIM GRAHAM

In his foreword to the 1998 *Green Paper Teachers – Meeting the Challenge of Change*, Tony Blair describes Labour's proposals as the 'most fundamental reform of the teaching profession since state education began...'. Does the Green Paper offer a coherent vision for 'meeting the challenge of change' for the C21st century learning society, or is it trapped in outmoded paradigms of instruction and obsolete bureaucracies of schooling? Does it deliver New Labour's public commitment to a more inclusive and democratic society or is it mired in the rut of nostrums inherited from the authoritarian outgoing Tory government and given a spin doctor makeover by closet control freaks for the shop window of media hype?

New Labour presents its ethical public policy as the conviction politics of a moral crusade, intended as a beacon of enlightenment at the turn of the millennium. But ministers have a pathological view of the teaching profession, in which teachers are not the victims of market reforms but the architects of their own fall from grace by their adherence to outmoded beliefs about autonomy, collegiality and progressivism. The sermonising tone is relentless – and if teachers are foolish enough to doubt the party doctrine for redemption, it is because they are poorly led, have an inadequate self image, low morale, a fatalistic outlook and a sense of despondency (para 23-4 of the Green Paper). Salvation, according to the Green Paper's tractarian evangelism, will be achieved only by abandoning the heresy of corrosive cynicism to follow a pilgrim's progress on the true path of New Labour's pedagogic and professional righteousness.

Sadly, many in education find such simple faith difficult to embrace, as the government's policy contradictions evoke inescapable skepticism. For example, teachers find it curious that radical restructuring of the profession should be proposed by government only a few weeks ahead of the establishment of a General Teaching Council which should be uniquely placed to generate democratic consensus. After all, say the government's critics, it has taken less time to devolve power to a Scottish parliament than to bring the General Teaching Council for England into existence, even in the circumscribed form which is the subject of current consultation.

Instead of setting up open systems to elicit ideas and to debate them, New Labour has chosen to promulgate a blueprint for re-engineering the profession, complete with an implementation schedule (para 176 of the Green Paper). Is this a deliberate attempt to pre-empt the legitimate terrain of negotiation, or is it merely political cynicism and inept change management? For a government elected on the manifesto of the Third Way in social democratic politics, it smacks of broken promises to teachers and the corruption of power.

New Labour boasts that its 'joined up thinking' gives rise to 'joined up government'. But closer interrogation of the details of the Green Paper, and analysis of the underpinning principles reveal a mass of inconsistencies and contradictions. Thus each of the commentaries in this volume engages with the challenge of change, and asks how far the government's proposed reforms represent workable and realistic strategies for the future. All of the contributions are polemical, and argue that the dissonances and discontinuities in the government's values and policies display major shortcomings which will need to be resolved if the aspirations to social justice and a world class education system are to be achieved.

John Tomlinson points up the need for democratic space in which authentic conversations about teaching and teacher professionalism can take place without the media circus of sloganising in adversarial politics. The General Teaching Council for England, which has been nurtured patiently to maturity by a committed coalition of educators, offers a unique window of opportunity to recapture professional cooperation and goodwill – but is inexplicably and unacceptably marginalised by the way the Green Paper has been orchestrated.

Peter Gilroy examines the proposals for the preparation and development of teachers, and finds that the reforms are counterproductive. Not only do they destabilise the carefully cultivated existing arrangements but their technical reductionist philosophy of training runs directly counter to the professionalisation of teaching expertise through higher education being adopted in countries whose educational achievements the government wishes to emulate.

Ann Campbell and **Ian Kane** consider the limitations of the proposals in the Green Paper for 'training schools', and the shortcomings of the apprenticeship model. Paradoxically, the government claims simultaneously that schools are inadequate, but that they provide the best location for teacher training; and that all schools should seek excellence, but that only a few will be supported to exemplify good practice for training purposes. Campbell and Kane contrast this misplaced elitism with the more inclusive and holistic approach to partnership between schools and universities, in which the full spectrum of teacher development can take place – co-ordinating programmes for beginning teaching, induction, and inservice with research, schoolbased teamwork and consultancy, community initiatives and interprofessional collaboration.

Stephanie Prestage and **Ann Williams** study the Green Paper proposals for induction of newly qualified teachers in the light of recent pilot programmes, research findings and emerging professional recommendations for good practice. They conclude that, despite the claims about balancing pressure and support to sustain the profession in achieving new levels of capability, the new induction procedures are largely punitive. The proposals are dominated by mechanisms to exclude potentially weak teachers at the expense of strategies to design programmes of professional development providing progression from ITT which are flexibly adapted to local and individual circumstances.

Ian Menter identifies the Green Paper's silences on matters of race and social justice. Although New Labour generally protests its egalitarian credentials by claiming all its policies are geared to social inclusion, the apparatus for the recruitment and training of new teachers gives rise to what can only be described (in the aftermath of the Lawrence Inquiry) as institutionalised racism. Ethnic minorities are grossly underrepresented in the teaching force, while the government still presides over structural obstacles in the form of regulations determining ethnocentric selection criteria and curricula. Advising teacher trainers to 'break the mould' when government itself erects the barriers, shows how little awareness of there is of the dynamics of exclusion. Menter concludes that the Green Paper has no credible vision of a teaching profession which properly reflects Britain as a multi-ethnic, multilingual and multi-cultural society taking its place in Europe or the wider world.

Les Bell takes issue with the model of headteacher as hero innovator and the hierarchical leadership assumptions explicit in the Green Paper's proposals for performance management. He points up the contradictions of rigid management styles for future uncertainty, and the need for collaborative working in flatter organisations which foster professional decision making and problem solving. Collective responsibility and empowerment, not individualised accountability and disempowerment, are the basic requirements for meeting the challenge of change.

John Trushell traces the shifts from old professionalism and old accountabilities to the new professionalism and new accountabilities under New Labour. He questions whether the translation of teachers from guides and mentors in the learning process to the new technocrats managing performance in learning outcomes, will appeal to potential graduate recruits choosing from the variety of careers available in the knowledge professions.

Louise Morley follows the arguments about performance management and the re-engineering of the profession into the literature about surface and deep level of reform. The discourse of standardisation, standards and measurement of educational outcomes overlays a more fundamental cultural shift towards the normalisation of technical rationality, acceptance of market relations, and internalisation of self-monitoring to comply with government performativity requirements. Any alternative view of professionalism, such as critical reflection and the engagement with other paradigms of education, becomes labelled as reactionary and anti-modernising.

Naz Rassool takes up a similar theme to highlight the evacuation of ethical and affective perspectives on teaching from the debate on professionalism. Instead, the Green Paper constructs teachers as competent technicians who deliver high-reliability school systems, programmed by scientifically-validated expert knowledge. Total Quality Management maintains constant surveillance of the effectiveness, efficiency and economy of these systems. The research base of such a restricted concept of professionalism is limited to the refining and transplanting of authorised knowledge.

My editorial conclusion addresses the confusions and inconsistencies in cognate strands of government policy. Schooling for vocational purposes continues to be equated with education, despite other more holistic policies about lifelong learning, citizenship and social inclusion. New Labour maintains a high level of state intervention in schooling, but gives explicit policy commitment to a light touch in other areas of endeavour in the knowledge-based economy. With the dismantling of the welfare state and the marketisation of education, the post-welfarist teacher is redefined as a technician in educational production – but nonetheless, 'welfarist' professional ideology of teaching as an altruistic vocation is mythologised in the recruitment advertisements designed to stem the catastrophic drop in recruitment to the profession. Without new teachers, the government's ambitious targets for raising educational standards will founder – but the low trust, high surveillance culture engendered by the Green Paper reforms make teaching much less attractive than other professions which offer more autonomy and global mobility.

Taken together, analyses which follow in this volume provide a powerfully argued counterpoint to the government's tokenistic consultation and assiduous media management of the respecification of teacher professionalism. Teachers' disappointment with New Labour has been its unwillingness to enter into genuine debate, preferring to stage manage set piece 'conferences' and to issue carefully phrased questionnaires which strictly control what may be negotiated and what may not. Ministers dismiss legitimate criticism as 'whingeing'. While infantilising the opposition may make good sound bites for the right wing press, it neither resolves the basic contradictions nor inspires confidence in the democratic process. Teachers who resist the imposition of the Green Paper proposals are portrayed as dinosaurs denying the march of progress, or latter-day Luddites locked in a time-warp. But as this collection amply demonstrates, there are fundamental structural weaknesses in New Labour's policies that deserve serious review. These fault-lines are the dilemmas of the nation state as it modernises in the new global economic order, and the essential arguments are likely to persevere long after the Green Paper has been consigned to the recycling bin of history.

CREATING DEMOCRATIC SPACE FOR DECISION-MAKING IN EDUCATION
THE ROLE OF THE GENERAL TEACHING COUNCIL

JOHN TOMLINSON
UNIVERSITY OF WARWICK

Government has come to control in fine detail the curriculum for schools and training teachers, and the methods of assessment and inspection of schools, teachers and LEAs. It is now proposing a major restructuring of the teaching profession, introducing competition for pay into school staffrooms whereas all the wisdom of school effectiveness shows that schools work best where team spirit is strongest.

Yet after thirty years – a generation of adults and six of schoolchildren – of this growing central grip there is still disquiet about school standards and an increasing problem of recruiting enough teachers. It must be time to ask whether all the nostrums of Conservatives and New Labour (almost indistiguishable in education policy) can deliver the goods needed for a learning-based economy and a pluralist society.

The burden of this essay is that part of the problem is that we have no means by which either the profession or the public can ask such questions and hope to get well-informed discussion which might lead to change if enough of us wanted it. Put in terms of the health of our civil society, the question is, *Where is the democratic space in which discussion of education policy can take place and have its legitimate effect upon the governors?*

All the instruments and organisations of the so-called period of consensus from the 1940s to the 1970s have been demolished as representing and supporting a corporatist and middle-of -the-road approach which is at the same time is too frail and too cumbersome to serve the need for sharp and rapid responses to face global competition and never-ending change. Now, where government, or more usually, one of its agencies, issues consultation documents the outcome is already foreclosed. Consultation and comment are confined to the agenda and proposals being put forward. The earlier stage, of asking what we want to achieve and inventing and reviewing several options for doing it, has either been set aside in favour of a preferred dogma or has already taken place behind closed doors. This in turn creates a situation in which those who may suggest alternatives are characterised as being against the objectives, when it is the process they would wish to have different. An all-or-nothing, those-who-are-not-for-us-are-against-us mentality thus arises and in the polarised atmosphere that follows even less improvement is achieved.

There are serious and intellectually respectable reasons for thinking that the education of our children has become over-prescribed and the schools too enmeshed in the language of targets, inspection and league tables. Those who think thus are not arguing against high standards and vibrant schools. Quite the contrary. But they are concerned at the growing evidence of a dysfunctional anxiety among pupils, teachers – and many parents. The structural problem for our education system is that this anxiety remains free-floating because there is no accepted way in which it can be rationally examined, and either shown to be groundless or, if it is not, lead to changes that will improve the lives of children.

Maybe it is not too late. There are interesting aspects of government policy and behaviour which could be the seeds of a more open education society. The review of the National Curriculum for schools, to take effect in 2000, will reinstate a place for social and personal education. That cannot happen unless teachers are trained and encouraged to think of children as persons as well as brains. Education Action Zones could show new ways to achieve educational objectives free of some of the uniformity generally imposed on schools, LEAs and teacher trainers. The Green Paper's concept of career-long professional development for teachers, meeting both the aims of the system and the need for continuing personal education, is a long hoped-for necessity, first proposed in the White Paper of 1972. And, most notable of all, the creation of a General Teaching Council, which will be operative from summer 2000. It is worthwhile reflecting on the opportunities for creating what I have called *democratic space* which the GTC will have. It will carry a grave responsibility to behave responsibly, so that the opportunities are not squandered. The profession has waited for more than a century for a government with the imagination and understanding to legislate a General Teaching Council.

The General Teaching Council will have responsibilities extending across teachers' qualifications, the registration of those eligible to teach, the supply of teachers, their initial training, the induction of newly qualified teachers, continuing professional development, re-training, professional discipline, public relations, and research related to all these matters, all of which are seen to be inseparable.

Let me take the issue of teacher supply to illustrate the difference the GTC could make. The Council will have a duty to advise the Secretary of State on the numbers needed for entry to ITT to implement public policy for the education service. The advice would need to cover national totals, age-phase and curricular areas and the most appropriate modes of training and re-training. To do this, the Council would need access to the continuing resource of government statistics and models for forecasting teacher supply. For the first time, all of this will be in the public domain. The Council will also be capable to investigate these questions on its own initiative, draw upon the statistics of teachers generated by its keeping of the Register, develop its own computer models as necessary, and make comment to government and others as it thinks appropriate. Crucially, it would make its recommendations in the context of the known age-structure of the profession, so that a long-term strategy would be possible. Targets subsequently approved by government for entry to training each year could be seen by the public in the light of all this information in a way that is not possible now. In effect, the GTC would be the regulatory body to advise on adequacy of supply and on notions of shortage (open, hidden or suppressed) or surplus.

The legitimacy of the GTC will be based on the fact that it will be a body which uniquely brings together the teaching profession as a whole (FE and

HE will be represented though the focus will be on schools) with central government, employing authorities and those immediately served by the schools. It is an opportunity to re-learn some of the political wisdom of the age of consensus because it would seem to be common-sense that since those who would ultimately have to take political decisions will be involved in GTC deliberations, it should be clear to the Council what are the parameters of the politically possible. Such a responsible approach in general would make all the more telling those few occasions when a difference of view with the government of the day had to be declared. It is not an impossible dream. The Advisory Council on the Supply and Education of Teachers (ACSET) resumed the work of a earlier similar body (ACSTT) set up following the recommendations of the Weaver and James Committees. Despite internal difficulties, it generated its own professional dynamic and made such clear recommendations for the future the then Secretary of State gave that as his reason for not reconvening it – it had given DES work for a decade.

ACSET was the last representative body for the education service.

> *It was unwieldy, over-dependent upon the DES and its inadequate information, and limited to responding to the questions which the government chose to ask. It did manage, however, to engage the whole maintained education service in deliberating together with central and local government on important questions of supply and training, and its recommendations still stand, some of them awaiting satisfactory response.* (Sayer, 1993).

In short it demonstrated the potential benefits the GTC could bring.

In Scotland there has been a GTC since 1966. In 1992-93 the Scottish Office undertook a policy review of the GTC. Its conclusions in relation the advice on teacher supply are relevant to the prospect for England:

> *The close match between the qualifications of Scottish teachers and the subjects they are required to teach stands in sharp contrast to the position in England and Wales where there is no equivalent of the General Teaching Council. This impressive correlation between qualifications held and tuition given is due in no small part to the Council's influence. It must be recognised that, were there no such body, the*

retention of this level of control would be extremely difficult and standards in Scottish education would be at risk...

Here is control which is both effective and accepted because it was devised co-operatively and serves ends all support. The Report continues:

...any developments proposed are discussed in a collaborative environment and are likely to receive more positive reception than would be the case were a Government department seeking to impose topdown changes.

What is described here for teacher supply would also be applicable to the entry standards required of teachers and the curriculum for initial teacher training where the GTC will have a duty to advise the Secretary of State. Likewise, the induction of new teachers and the continuing professional development of teachers are matters on which the GTC will advise the Secretary of State, whereas, at present, the remit for both policy and action lies de facto with the Teacher Training Agency. A better balance between policy formation (by government, profession and public representation) and policy implementation (by government or its agencies) can be envisaged.

In the next twelve months most of the decisions crucial to the success or failure of the General Teaching Council will be made: the appointment of the Chief Executive, the budget for the first three years, its location, the elections and appointments to the Council and all the DfEE Regulations translating the intentions of Parliament into administrative procedures.

The whole education service, and especially teachers, need to be aware of the opportunities to share in policy making that are being opened. It is the chance not of a lifetime, but of a century.

THE THREAT TO UNIVERSITY-BASED TEACHER EDUCATION

PETER GILROY

UNIVERSITY OF SHEFFIELD

Stupidity does not consist in being without ideas... Human Stupidity consists in having lots of ideas, but stupid ones.
(Henry de Montherlant, *Notebooks*)

Introduction

It could easily be assumed from press reports and the emphasis that the title of the Green Paper gives to teachers that the proposals it contains will only affect school teachers. This view would be confirmed by the two forewords by Blair and Blunkett as these emphasise the radical nature of the proposals and have a clear focus on school teachers, with no mention of teacher educators. However, a hint of the wider implications of the proposals can be seen in Blunkett's Press Release concerning the Green Paper (3.12.98) when he says that 'we want to improve teacher training (sic)' and continues by stating that in addition to the national curriculum for initial teacher training there will be 'new national tests for all trainee teachers in numeracy, literacy and ICT...We plan to establish a network of training schools to share innovation and good practice in school-led teacher training'.

It would appear that there is little here to concern teacher educators, other than the additional work that will be involved with organising the 'new national tests for all trainee teachers in numeracy, literacy and ICT', which seem to be in addition to current requirements, and convincing new applicants that they are worthwhile.

The serious implications of the Green Paper's proposals for University Departments of Education (UDEs) and the teaching profession as a whole only become clear when one reads Chapter 4, 'Better Training'. Recently, a series of dubiously motivated so-called 'reforms' of initial and in-service teacher education have seriously destabilised UDEs' provision, with a concomitant effect on teacher supply and the range of courses available to support teachers' continued professional development. I wish to argue that if all of Chapter 4's proposals were put into practice then they have the potential to take the process of destabilisation still further, to the extent that they could destroy university-based provision altogether. First, however, I need to identify quite what it is that the Green Paper's proposals are supposed to be 'bettering'.

1848-1969: From Under-Qualified To Qualified Professionals

Up until 1848 there was little or no formal teacher education in Britain. In fact at the elementary schools the older pupils themselves acted as teachers. A very small number of these 'pupil-teachers' moved on to religious colleges to study for a teacher's certificate, a qualification that was introduced in 1848. However, the vast majority of teachers simply learned almost as apprentices how to teach, in effect 'learning on the job'. In 1861 a government enquiry into this state of affairs (the Newcastle Commission) concluded that this system was failing both the teachers and their pupils and eventually it was recommended by the government that universities should be involved with teacher education (see Patrick *et al.*, 1982). By 1947 colleges of education provided much of initial teacher education, with university departments of education supervising the quality of these college-based courses. This system seemed to work well, in that it 'had the effect of both strengthening and broadening the professional and academic aspects of training' (Gosden, 1989, p.2), a role that even Her Majesty's Inspectorate (HMI) identified as 'significant' (DES, 1988a, p.1).

The complex work of educating trainee teachers being carried out by the colleges required them to extend their courses from two, to three, to four years, with the fourth year being introduced in 1963 so as to allow the colleges to offer a B.Ed. qualification to their student teachers. By the beginning of the 1970s it would have been difficult to find a new teacher who was not also a graduate. The government's Department of Education and Science (DES[1]) have recently published statistics which show the growth of the graduate profession very clearly (DES, 1991, p.38). According to these figures there was a six-fold increase in elementary school teacher graduates between 1972 and 1988 (from 5% to 30%) and almost a doubling of secondary school teacher graduates in the same period (from 37% to 63%). The important point to note from these figures and the developments outlined above is that the idea that teachers could in some strange way acquire their professional knowledge simply by working in schools and somehow picking up the complex skills of teaching without a major contribution from universities and colleges was something that had been left behind in the dim and distant Victorian past.

1970-1991: The Rising Storm

The government began to turn its attention to initial teacher education in 1970 with the publication of the James Report (DES, 1972). Only one of the report's recommendations, the introduction of an induction programme for new teachers in their probationary year, was implemented, but with hindsight it can be seen as the first time that a late twentieth century British government felt able to dictate policy and practice to teacher educators. There followed a whole forest of reports from the DES and HMI. In the main these were very complimentary about the way in which initial teacher education was being organised, with one report, for example, pointing out that schools were only dissatisfied with a mere 4% of new teachers (DES, 1988b, p.59). However, it was as a result of these reports (in particular the report which examined the nature of initial teacher education – DES, 1983) that in 1984 the government created a new body, the Council for the Accreditation of Teacher Education (CATE), whose role was to approve courses of teacher education.

For the universities in particular this was a double shock. First the autonomy of university education departments was clearly threatened. Previously, like any department in a British university, education departments had been masters of their own destiny. They had the freedom to create courses, validate courses in other institutions and keep outsiders, such as the government, at arm's length. Now, however, if they continued in this way and refused to allow CATE to inspect their initial teacher education courses then the courses would not be approved and so students would not be accepted as qualified teachers. Inevitably the courses would not be able to recruit students and would close.

Secondly, it gradually became clear that the government, not the universities, now controlled initial teacher education. Membership of the all-important CATE was solely in the hands of the education minister and it soon became clear that professional educators would be very much in the minority. Despite the very positive reports on teacher education from the government's own professional advisors (see above, DES, 1988b) the government, in particular the minister responsible for education, seemed to view those responsible for teacher education with a 'lack of trust, even suspicion' (Gosden, 1989, p.9).

1991-1995: The Storm Breaks

In January of 1992 the then minister for education, Kenneth Clarke, gave a speech at the North of England Annual Education Conference. In it his rejection of university-based teacher education, even that supervised by CATE, became clear. He laid out plans to hand over the one-year secondary initial teacher education course to schools[2], to the extent that at least 80% of a student's time would be school-based (four days a week), which would require a 'considerable shift of funds' from universities and colleges to the schools (Clarke, 1992, p.13). Other types of initial teacher education course would eventually follow this school-based pattern, but the one year secondary course would have to change with effect from September 1992.

It became quite clear that these radical changes to initial teacher education had been created with little or no understanding of their implications, other than the fact that universities and colleges would have their contact with students drastically reduced. There were two kinds of criticism to be levelled against these changes. The first pointed out that the only real justification for implementing such radical and rapid change would be to show that existing forms of initial teacher education were in some sense failing adequately to prepare students for the profession. Self-appointed right-wing think tanks did attempt to argue such a case. For example, one of this group presented a series of assertions which claimed that higher education courses of teacher education provide 'spurious and questionable studies' with 'no solid grounding in the real world' (O'Hear, 1988, p.6), culminating in the slur that, by implication, all those involved with teaching such courses were neo-Marxists (*ibid.*, p.23). In direct contradiction, the minister's own professional advisors had reported that, although there was always room for improvement, much of the work carried out by those concerned with initial teacher education was more than satisfactory (DES, 1991). Where was the rational justification for these changes which appeared to be turning the clock back to the 1800s?

Secondly, a whole host of practical problems were identified (see Gilroy, 1992). Perhaps the most important to a government very aware of the need to control expenditure was the fact that on their own figures the cost of such a change were prohibitive. A two-year school-based course (the Articled Teacher scheme) had recently been introduced as a pilot and it seemed that the minister wanted all courses to develop in this way. Yet government costings showed that this was impossible without considerable expense. The total cost in 1992 of bringing both the B.Ed. and the PGCE courses within the Articled Teacher Scheme would have been more than £452 million, an increase of more than £80 million over the 1990/91 initial teacher education budget. If this extra money were not found then initial teacher education would be seriously underfunded and in fact no more than £6 million was actually made available for the transition, this lack of funds eventually being singled out as a significant problem by successive chairmen of the Parliamentary Select Committee on Education (see Gilroy, Price, Stones and Thornton, 1994, p.293).

Then there were the practical problems. How would more than 24,000 student teachers be easily fitted into schools for four days per week without seriously disrupting the schools' own work? A survey of head teachers in schools found that not one agreed with these proposals (TES[3], 31.1.92), with another head teacher quoted as saying that she was deeply concerned that school-based initial teacher education would 'degenerate into an uncoordinated series of experiences within schools' (TES, 21.2.92). Finally, the universities themselves were opposed to the scheme as they did not see how they could validate a course which was organised in such a way that they could only see students for at most one day per week (CVCP[4], 1992). Moreover, it seemed extraordinarily wasteful to require the university teacher educators to train school teachers (CATE, 1992) in order that the school teachers could then do the job that had previously been carried out by the university teacher educators.

None of these criticisms were answered. After the General Election of 1992 the only major change in this area implemented by the new minster for education, Mr. Patten, was a reduction of the requirement for 80% of school-based work to 66% (that is, students on the one-year PGCE course would be in schools for 24 weeks out of 36). It was clear that with Patten's principle that 'money should follow the student' into school (Patten, 1992, p.2) university departments of education would be hard pressed financially. In fact the director of one well known existing school-based course offered by Sussex university explained that it was likely that for financial reasons the course would have to close down (TES, 3.7.92).

One year later Mr Patten announced the way in which he was going to resolve the funding issue. He would create a new Teacher Training Agency, which would replace CATE. It would draw its funds from money that had previously been allocated directly to the universities' funding body. It was originally proposed that not only would this new Agency be responsible for initial teacher education, it would also control research higher degrees in education and research in education. In this way the government, through the Agency, would control virtually all aspects of teacher education, especially as the Agency would be responsible for inspecting teacher education courses through a body that was responsible for school inspections, the Office for Standards in Education (OFSTED).

The criticism of these proposals was virtually unanimous, with the powerful Committee of Vice-chancellors and Principals threatening to withdraw from initial teacher education and pointing out that these changes were a 'serious threat to quality and would lead to an increase in political control', as well as damaging the independence and quality of educational research (TES, 5.11.93). Just as significant was the publication of a response by the retiring chair of CATE, Professor Taylor. He argued that there were three principles that any change in teacher education should be measured against, namely, as compared to what already exists, will the new system:

1. attract good candidates?

2. produce better educated and more competent teachers?

3. provide a sound basis for continued professional development?

He concluded that the new proposals failed 'on all three counts' (THES[5], 22.10.93).

It seems likely that as with many of the previous, Conservative, government's educational reforms, the new system of teacher education was only able to operate because of the immense goodwill and professionalism of school teachers and teacher educators. The partnerships between schools and university education departments were well in place long before 1992 and were based not so much on financial considerations as on the shared desire to prepare students as effectively as possible for their profession (see Barber, 1993). It is these partnerships that seem to be the key to making school-based initial teacher education effective and yet, for the reasons already touched upon, it is these partnerships that are most under strain. The cracks are beginning to appear with, on the one hand universities preparing to withdraw altogether from initial teacher education (see Gilroy, Price, Stones and Thornton, 1994, pp.287-288 and TES, 27.12.94, p.5) and on the other hand schools too rethinking their commitment to this form of teacher education (TES, 19.5.95).

If one adds to this bleak picture the fact that applications for the current teacher education courses had, by comparison with applications for the 1996-97 cohort, again fallen (the four-year B.Ed. courses are down by 15%, secondary PGCE courses by 10.85% and primary courses by 4.66% – TES 6.2.98) then the true results of the yet-to-be-justified 'reform' of initial teacher education can be seen. The politicians' attacks on teachers and teacher educators, supported by what have been termed 'the fanatics' of the ill-informed New Right (Whitty, 1993, p.274), have created a situation whereby the present and future forms of initial teacher education seem to echo the systems of the past. The inevitable result has been the rupturing of the delicate links between higher education and the schools, links that both of these contributors to teacher education clearly find both valuable and absolutely necessary to a proper preparation for the profession of teaching. The new Labour government has yet to do anything which shows that it recognises the devastating impact that its predecessor's ill-considered 'reforms' have had upon the teaching profession and, ultimately, our children.

Most English university education departments have two elements to their teaching. It is the 'reform' of the first, initial teacher education, which I have so far described here. However the other element, in-service education for experienced teachers (INSET) is also under threat. In 1997 the Teacher Training Agency was allowed by the new Labour government to turn its attention to INSET provision. Because universities have in the main offered various post-graduate qualifications (such as advanced diplomas and masters degrees) to teachers who successfully complete their university INSET studies a substantial amount of funding (approximately thirty million pounds) was provided by the Higher Education Funding Council (HEFCE), in exactly the same way that HEFCE provided funding for other university work. In the summer of 1997 the Agency attempted with some success to take over that funding from HEFCE on the grounds that it was the Agency and not HEFCE that was responsible for teacher training. It identified eight areas that would receive INSET funding and required university education departments to bid for those funds. Those bids were then judged by a panel appointed by the Agency, with the results being released in February 1998. It was also announced that those university departments of education which had refused to hand over their HEFCE INSET funding to the Agency would have to suffer the indignity of being audited so as to confirm their claim that the work they were doing was not part of the Agency's conception of INSET.

Thus, as with the initial teacher education context, the INSET context into which the Green Paper's proposals are placed is also a seriously destabilised one. To begin with university education departments have lost their ability to work with experienced teachers so as to identify their professional needs and offer graduate level programmes of continued professional development. Instead they must follow whatever the Agency has identified as being worthy of funding. In addition education departments must meet criteria for being accepted for funding Agency INSET or receive no funding whatsoever. The result has been catastrophic. 36 education departments did not have their INSET bids accepted, so teachers in large areas of the country which they serve will have no INSET whatsoever and the Open University, for example, who serve the country as a whole has lost almost one and a half million pounds of INSET funds. Staff who taught on both INSET and initial teacher education courses might have to be made redundant, with further knock-on negative effects to initial teacher education courses.

What I have outlined here is the development of a centralisation of initial and post-experience teacher education. All that the future seems to offer is initial and post-experience teacher education separated from the university system that was once seen as so important in raising the quality and standards of the profession with control passing in a rigidly centralised way to a government organisation. Indeed the Agency's chief executive has stated publicly that 'initial teacher education is not an academic study; and therefore an intrinsic part of higher education' (THES, 18.4.97). This might mean that initial teacher education should not consist of purely theoretical academic study and who could disagree with that? However the actual practice of the Agency prior to the publication of the Green Paper shows that the future of teacher education (both initial and post-experience) would appear not to be one that necessarily involves higher education.

The Green Paper, in particular Chapter 4, represents an opportunity to reverse the trends of the last decade or so and to reverse some of the damaging 'reforms' introduced by the previous government. I will now turn to comment on particular paragraphs of the Green Paper to see if that opportunity has been grasped.

The Green Paper and Initial Teacher Education

We intend to review the funding arrangements (for ITE) to ensure that they recognise the role of schools as equal partners. In particular, we will consult on the case for funding higher education/school partnerships directly rather than channelling funding for partner schools through higher education institutions. (DfEE, 1998, para. 110)

This represents a direct threat to current funding arrangements for ITE. If it means that schools will receive funds directly and then purchase whatever 'ITE services' they require from UDEs then there would seem to be little or no understanding of the importance of the consistency required of those 'services' for all student teachers, as the UDE element of their ITE course could vary from school to school. On the other hand it could mean that these 'higher education/school partnerships' would have their own funds, managed quite separately from the universities' own arrangements and the result could well be a re-creation of the college training system (that is, initial teacher education funded separately from other university provision). At the very least universities might then wonder why they should continue to house and subsidise such partnerships.

> *Alongside the existing one-year certificate we propose to develop new modular courses for postgraduate teacher training available from 2000, structured in shorter segments and with flexible start and end points.* (DfEE, 1998, para. 112)

> *When the new modules are available we will ask higher education institutions to look at ways of integrating teacher training modules into their undergraduate degrees so that students could gain experience and recognition by working as paid associates in school while taking the relevant modules of the teaching course...Such approaches will increasingly break down the barriers between undergraduate and postgraduate training.* (DfEE, 1998, para. 113)

It is unclear who will in fact 'develop' these courses, but although para. 112 might well attract mature graduates into the profession the detail as to how their school placements will operate is not explained, nor how these might impact on the PGCE course itself. Paragraph113 is more puzzling, as the immediately preceding paragraph the Green Paper states, 'We are already seeing a move away from the undergraduate study of education (through the Bachelor of Education degree course) to more postgraduate training' (para. 112), yet this proposal seems to recreate the B.Ed., albeit with the academic element based in subject departments. One wonders whether subject departments would be happy to allow their students to extend their course so that they can work 'as paid associates in a school' and also what PGCE students on a grant will think of non-graduates being paid 'while taking the relevant modules of the teaching course'.

> *We propose to introduce skills tests which trainees would have to pass before they could be awarded Qualified teacher Status (QTS). The test will be set and examined nationally and could be taken before, during or after training.* ((DfEE, 1998, para. 107)

Quite how this will attract students in to the profession, especially those who already meet the requirements in literacy and numeracy, is not made clear. We could have the ridiculous situation where an English or Mathematics graduate would have to take additional tests to prove their literacy or mathematical ability.

> *We will consult on ways of strengthening the assessment of individual trainees for QTS. One option would be for the Teacher Training Agency to accredit all external examiners of initial teacher training courses.* (DfEE, 1998, para. 109)

Leaving aside the assumption that current forms of assessment are in some way suspect, the implications this proposal has for the autonomy of universities are obvious. In addition one wonders how many external examiners would be prepared to offer themselves for accreditation by the Teacher Training Agency.

If all these proposals were to be accepted then I would suggest that they could result in the following scenario for ITE in the twenty-first century. Despite the fact that current School Centred Initial Teacher Training (SCITT) schemes are very expensive, receive very poor OFSTED reports and so, on the government's own criteria, cannot possibly compare in quality or quantity with one-year PGCE courses or four-year B.Ed. courses, the Green Paper's proposals will encourage something like these schemes to grow. Universities will see no reason to remain in the business of providing high quality initial professional education for teachers and the vacuum will be filled by school consortia, buying in whatever services they feel appropriate from universities or other providers. Running alongside these consortia could be provision in the form of subject departments in universities releasing undergraduate students from their subject studies for periods to study 'teacher training modules' and to work as paid associates in schools. All of these new student teachers will then have to take additional skills tests in numeracy and literacy.

The impact of the Green Paper's proposals on ITE represent a return to a situation where the hard-won situation of a profession prepared for their careers in schools by a well thought out form of partnership between school and university provision will be replaced with a jumble of SCITT and main subject department provision. Quite what UDE courses will then exist for the TTA's accredited external examiners to inspect remains unclear. Moreover, all these proposals are predicated on the assumption that there is something seriously at fault with current UDE provision, so serious that it has to be swept away. This assumption is never expressed clearly nor, of course, justified.

The Green Paper and the Continued Professional Development of Teachers

Much existing training is unsystematic and unfocussed. We intend to set out a clear framework for professional development which brings together national, school and individual training priorities to help all teachers to raise standards in the classroom and to progress within the new career structure. (DfEE, 1998, para. 122)

Where is the evidence to support the slur that is represented in the unjustified and unsupported assertion of the first sentence of this paragraph? The emphasis on 'training' as opposed to the continued professional development of teachers is also not justified. Teachers should be aware that they are having a Continued Professional Development (CPD) framework imposed on them, to the extent that even their 'individual development needs' are only to be recognised through a school-based appraisal (para. 123). This, of course, is precisely what is happening with the current TTA-INSET courses described earlier.

We believe that new quality assurance arrangements are needed... We will consult on a new Code of Practice for all major providers of publicly-funded training. It would, for example, require providers to reflect up-to-date research and inspection evidence, to link provision directly to the proposed new career structure, and to include mechanisms for monitoring and evaluating the impact on pupil performance. (DfEE, 1998, para. 125)

The Teaching and Higher Education Act gives OFSTED a new statutory right to inspect and report on the quality of any in-service training provided for school teachers from public funds. We intend to ask OFSTED, in consultation with the Teacher Training Agency, to draw up proposals for a rolling programme of inspection of existing provision... (DfEE, 1998, para. 126)

Paragraph 125 could have been written by the TTA, as its last sentence mimics the terminology used in the TTA-INSET documents. There is no justification given for the view that 'new quality assurance arrangements are needed' and those that are currently being introduced by OFSTED for TTA-INSET courses are, to say the least, suspect (for example, OFSTED have admitted that they have no idea how they are going to be able to monitor and evaluate the impact of TTA-INSET courses on the short or long term aspects of pupil performance). CPD would become tightly controlled by the TTA as provision would have to be linked 'directly to the proposed new career structure', so removing the opportunities that teachers would have to identify their own professional development.

The proposal that OFSTED and the TTA would have the legal right to 'inspect and report on the quality of any in-service training provided for school teachers from public funds' must also be questioned. It directly attacks the autonomy of universities, whilst assuming that OFSTED and the TTA are organisations that are effective in monitoring quality when all the evidence points in the other direction (see for example the criticisms currently being offered to the Select Committee on Education). It asserts, again without any evidence, that existing HEFCE quality assurance systems are unsatisfactory and would allow OFSTED and the TTA the legal right to inspect any university course, not just those in education departments, that could be identified as 'in-service training for teachers', thus adding a duplication of quality audits faced by those departments.

The picture being painted here is one that reflects the most recent attempts by the TTA to dictate, control and impose the form of professional development for teachers. As with the proposals for initial teacher education, if everything in the Green Paper became law then it would be the government, through the TTA, that identified teachers' in-service needs with some form of national curriculum for INSET being all that would be funded.

The question that has to be asked of this vision of the future is whether or not teachers want to hand over to the Agency the control they have of their own professional development. Furthermore, is this in fact the way that teachers want to develop professionally? Where is there opportunity for scholarly study in depth of critical policy and practice issues that concern teachers? All that the future, as promised by the Green Paper's proposals, seems to offer is initial and post-experience teacher education separated from the university system that was once seen as so important in raising the quality and standards of the profession, with control passing in a rigidly centralised way to a government organisation.

Concluding Remarks

It might appear from what I have presented here that I am opposed to everything in the Green Paper. However, there is much that I would welcome. For example, the identification of the CPD needs of supply teachers (127), the idea that learning accounts be used to support teachers taking MA and doctoral degrees (129), the possibility of scholarships and sabbaticals for teachers (134), are all proposals that would be hard to fault. But there is also a very great deal that has to be challenged.

The title of Chapter 4 is 'Better Training', carrying with it two assumptions: the first is that in spite of all that has been done to improve teacher education it is still somehow seriously flawed and the second is that the proposal in the Green Paper would create a situation where there was 'better' provision for teacher education than currently exists. My argument here has been that neither of these assumptions are sound. Chapter 4 is predicated on the belief that most of what is proposed are undisputed reforms to a failing system of teacher education. However, current forms of initial teacher education offered through university/school partnership system and existing forms of continued professional development found alongside provision focussed more sharply on government needs, have still to be shown to be failing. It seems clear that what is proposed for teacher education in the Green Paper would lead the profession back to a system that was for good reason rejected more than a century ago. It would be a supreme and tragic irony if in 'meeting the challenge of change' New Labour missed the opportunity that the Green Paper provides to build on the considerable strengths of the present system and reject once and for all unjustified Victorian Conservative 'reforms' to teacher education.

References

Barber, M. (1993) 'The truth about partnership', *Journal of Education for Teaching*, vol. 19, no.3, pp.255-262.

Clarke, K. (1992) *Speech to the North of England Education Conference*, mimeo.

DES (1972), *Teacher Education and Training*, James Report, London, HMSO.

DES (1983) *Teaching in Schools: the context of initial teacher training*, London, HMSO.

DES (1988a) *Education Observed*, London, DES.

DES (1988b) *The New Teacher in School*, London, HMSO.

DES (1991) *School-based Initial Teacher Training in England and Wales*, London, HMSO.

Gilroy, D. P. (1992) 'The political rape of initial teacher education in England and Wales: a JET rebuttal', *Journal of Education for Teaching*, vol.18, no.1, pp.5-22.

Gilroy, D. P., Price, C., Stones, E. and Thornton, M. (1994) 'Teacher Education in Britain: a JET symposium with politicians', *Journal of Education for Teaching*, vol.20., no.3, 1994, pp.261-300.

Gosden, P. H. J. H (1989) 'Teaching quality and the accreditation of initial teacher-training courses', in: V. A. McClelland and V. P. Varma (Eds.) *Advances In Teacher Education,* London, Routledge, pp.1-18.

O'Hear, A. (1988) *Who Teaches the Teachers?*, Research Report 10, London, The Social Affairs Unit.

Patrick, H., Bernbaum, G. and Reid, K. (1982) *The Structure and Process of Initial Teacher Education Within Universities in England and Wales*, Leicester, University of Leicester School of Education.

Patten, J. (1992) *Letter to Sir William Taylor,* Chairman, CATE mimeo.

Whitty, G. (1993) 'Education reform in England in the 1990s', in Gilroy, D. P. and Smith, M. (Eds.), *International Analyses of Teacher Education*, Oxford, Carfax, pp.263-275.

Notes

1 The DES became the Department of Education (DfE) and subsequently The Department for Education and Employment (DfEE).

2 Until 1992 there were basically two routes into teaching, one through the four-year Bachelor of education (B.Ed), the other for graduates through the one-year Post-graduate Certificate in Education (PGCE).

3 *The Times Educational Supplement.*

4 Committee of Vice-chancellors and Principals.

5 *Times Higher Education Supplement*

STUDYING NEXT TO NELLIE
AN EXPLORATION OF
'TRAINING SCHOOLS'

ANNE CAMPBELL AND IAN KANE
MANCHESTER METROPOLITAN UNIVERSITY

The notion of 'training school' as postulated in the Green Paper (1998) could be an interesting one. However, the way it is being 'spun' is disappointing and could be another piece of evidence for those who charge that the current government's preoccupation is with image and appearance rather than anything more substantial. The 'training school' concept would appear to be a development of the earlier notion of the 'laboratory school' first run in the manifesto and the White Paper. It was unclear then what a laboratory school might be other than a well-resourced clinical setting linked in to the National Grid for Learning. Now what? Apparently resources are to be made available. Quite large sums of money could be targeted at the lucky schools who can demonstrate a clear mission to contribute to the preparation of the next generation of teachers, and who see such work as part of their core business. There is talk of satellite schools and of staff specially recruited because of their commitment and skills in the area of work with intending teachers. Training school? One could offer the alternative designation: Training College circa 1944-1964. The definition of a training school and other characteristics of this brainchild of a government seeking to 'break the mould', would seem to include no guaranteed place for higher education – otherwise all one might get, it is seemingly feared by central government and its advisers, is 'superpartnership' schools. Nor, however, are they seen as super School Centred Initial Teacher Training Scheme Schools (SCITTS) either – a plague on both houses. The government unsurprisingly is looking for something new.

Their pursuit of innovation should be guided by the old adage, offering advice on babies and bathwater.

The baby in this case is the now well-established concept of partnership. Certainly it is not SCITT. One wonders what a 'super SCITT' would be. It seems a contradiction in terms. A study of grades awarded to SCITT schools after Office for Standards in Education (OFSTED) inspection reveals, at the time of writing – January 1999 – a single grade 1 cell in the entire country. Let us be clear about this data. A cell is not a Teacher Training Agency (TTA) category. A cell is one of six (secondary) or fourteen (primary) headings under which grades are awarded. One SCITT (of dozens in the country) has achieved one Grade 1 in one cell. That cell was Selection – in practice, the least significant of all secondary grades. By contrast Bishop Grossette College in Lincoln achieved in the Primary Follow Up Survey (PFUS) 12 Grade 1s, 1 Grade 2 and 1 Grade 3. This did not save it from being placed in quality Category C by the TTA because of the malign Grade 3 cell. Grade 3 is the commonest grade in SCITT schemes – ie the grade most often awarded. It is hard to see training school butterflies emerging from the chrysalis of SCITTs.

On the other hand it is hard to see where else they would come from other than established partnerships. One has to ask what could possibly be wrong with a 'super-partnership' school? Partnership as a formal notion has been around for 7 years now (officially launched January 4 1992, in Kenneth Clarke's speech to the North of England conference at Southport). During that time some schools have shone out as beacons – models of good and evolving practice. In the Manchester secondary partnership there are approximately 200 schools. Whilst the majority have few ambitions to be more than good and conscientious placement partners, seeing ITT as no real part of their core business, perhaps as many as 20% have demonstrated a broader interest and a wider vision. They offer specialist training facilities eg. in ICT, beyond the resources of their higher education partner. They seek to marry the lessons and tasks of teacher preparation with a broader professional development role and they do this in conjunction with higher education. There are many ways of exploring potential. The broader role sought could embrace NQTs, often on a programme leading to certification or it could mean a number of staff enhancing their qualifications at the university, or even in two cases through a school – based masters programme. Or it could mean in other cases, the banking of in-service funds with the university, to provide a brokering service – often using other partnership schools – to set up a programme for the year, designed to meet identified and negotiated needs. Or it could mean collaborating with higher education in a school-based research project, leading to publications and research degrees. Whichever road to broader development is chosen, it matters fundamentally that the school is a *partnership* school, that is to say that it has been in the business of initial training for up to seven years evolving its thinking about the ramifications and extensions of that in sustained dialogue with colleagues in higher education.

In any case where else could training schools come from, given that SCITTs have proved to be a busted flush? Surely they will not be those schools which for seven years have stood aside from partnership, arguing that the presence of student teachers in the school would endanger their levels of academic attainment and/or frighten the horses. Some parents have shown themselves to be very hostile to the idea of having students teaching their children. Such schools incidentally have not been slow to seek to employ young teachers trained on the back of other schools. HMI intelligence, unpublished, but transmitted to a conference on mentoring in schools, in Oxford in April 1995, (see McIntyre and Hagger (1996) for reports of the research project), seemed to indicate that Newly Qualified Teachers (NQTs) in their first post fared better in schools which were in partnership than they did when recruited to schools which were not. This should not be a surprise for several reasons. Staff who are used to supporting and giving critical feedback to student teachers can transfer those skills to supporting NQTs. The existence of a school infrastructure which promotes collegiality by peer observation and review, team working and regular professional dialogue is a natural developmental environment. The involvement of staff engaged in researching their own practice as part of a school-based professional development action research course, aimed at managing change, can offer valuable support to NQTs engaging in self appraisal and review. Experience and recent research, Whiting *et al.* (1996) Campbell and Kane (1998) Bines and Welton (1995) tell us that it still remains the case that the vast majority of schools, both primary and secondary, want to be in partnership with HE, and *do not want* to go it alone. OFSTED evidence, as indicated, confirms overwhelmingly that it is the partnership style of provision which offers the highest quality training.

It is salutary to look at the emerging Professional Development Schools (PDS) in the USA. At first encounter these can seem to be little more than embryonic (let alone super) partnership schools and some are indeed little more than that, working with universities and colleges who see benefit in a more school-based programme – not true of all higher education in the USA.

However, the definition of a PDS takes us much further than that. Drawing upon American Association of Colleges of Teacher Education (AACTE) literature a PDS can be characterised as having to accomplish four purposes:

- Exemplary education for a segment of the student population

- A clinical setting for pre-service education

- Continuing Professional Development (CPD) for teachers and lecturers

- Enquiry and research that advances the knowledge of schooling.

One might also wish to consider 'lighthouses', another US notion which is beginning to involve the designation of certain teacher education providers as having a special role to support and link to centres of excellence of differing types, such as laboratory schools, beacon schools and PDS.

What comes through clearly is not only the CPD dimension already discussed but also a research dimension. This should not be thought of as something pretentious seeking to light up the blue skies. It is concerned with supporting teachers to enquire systematically into their own practice and to make the outcomes of such enquiries in some way public. It would certainly include notions of practitioner research and evidence-based practice, to cite two currently high profile aspects of research.

When one reads the literature of the growth of PDS which it must be stressed has not arisen from government 'fiat', it becomes apparent that things work because Higher Education (HE) wishes to shift the centre of gravity of teacher preparation closer to schools, that schools believe that this is right and beyond that, have their own aspirations in the areas of professional development and enquiry. Such a development was occurring in

England eg. the Oxford Internship scheme, before Clarke hi-jacked the notion. Be that as it may, in PDS/HE relationships a symbiotic relationship evolves and the schools positively welcome their links with HE, which they see as raising them to higher levels of status. Why else have some SCITTs tried to join the Universities Council for the Education of Teachers (UCET)? A training school which did not have a systematic attachment to a neighbouring university would be as logical as a teaching hospital divorced from a medical faculty. Let us applaud training schools but let us recognise that they can sensibly really only come from the organic growth of a partnership school into a 'super-partnership' school.

So far the model explored has been a secondary model. To what extent could a primary school or group of schools develop into a training school or training school complex? What could a primary training school look like? What have we learned from primary school-based teacher education that might contribute to the development of training schools? A cluster group of small primary schools in partnership with HE is not an unknown phenomenon and large primary schools already exist which effectively function as training schools in so far as they regularly have diverse groups of students being supported by staff in school who in turn are supported by tutors from HE. Mentoring in primary schools has evolved as something quite different from secondary school mentoring. Commonly, in primary schools the class teacher is a central player, who often both supports and assesses the student teacher. However, beyond that a variety of models exist up and down the country, influenced by such factors as school size, HE practices in the levels of collaboration with partners and the style of management of school-based elements of teacher education. Who does what in primary school-based teacher education is a complex and problematic area. It is not as simple as, sometimes governments or their Agencies have seemed to think, establishing a theory/practice divide or a division of labour. Whole school approaches are favoured by many partnerships, due to the potential continuing professional development for existing, experienced teachers. Schools' engagement in research as partners with HE tutors is also beginning to emerge as a powerful way to promote a research-based teaching profession. Edwards and Collison (1996) give examples of how teachers are co-researchers, as do Campbell and Kane (1998) in the Mentoring in Schools Project. Several Teacher

Training Agency (TTA) and Economic and Social Research Council (ESRC) projects, for example, at Manchester, Leeds, Lancaster and Exeter, aim to team tutors in partnership primary schools researching professional development on Literacy and Numeracy alongside teachers researching their own practice in those areas. So, already a model is developing which crosses the boundaries of teaching, supervising and researching. Education Action Zone (EAZ) developments in the Greater Manchester region, and no doubt elsewhere, are also full of promise for similar collaborative ventures. What we have learned from these ventures is that finding a single simple model is not easy. There is a synergy in the process. Schools and teachers need support from tutors who can develop practical research approaches suitable for hard pressed schools and teachers, which result in real improvements in the learning opportunities for pupils. This is a far cry from the 'ivory towers' notion of research and scholarly activity. Could 'training schools' take on these approaches and develop them? If the challenges presented by these collaborative ventures in both primary and secondary sectors are successfully met, and taken on board by schools and universities, we can look forward to the development of lifelong professional development for teachers at all stages of their careers and provide for those advanced skills teachers, professional challenges in their classrooms which are built upon collaboration with colleagues in school and HE. The springboard for much of this activity is mutual collaboration in initial teacher education and training. However, heed must be taken also of the pressures put on schools by their involvement in initial teacher education. Downes (1996) identifies the following 'problems' for schools; pressure on physical space of staffrooms and classrooms; pressure on staff to 'perform' well in front of students; parental fear of a dropping of standards or of experimentation with their offspring; novices devouring precious resources; additional stress for teachers with regard to their students' lack of progress; and the costing of time against income received for mentoring.

As outlined above, a case can be powerfully argued for encouraging training schools to develop from partnership – but there is another dimension to the argument. The opposite of partnership is not SCITT – because most SCITT schemes do associate themselves, to greater or lesser degree with higher education. The true opposite of partnership is 'on-the-job training'.

This can be dressed up in all sort of ways. In England maximum credibility is bestowed by the title Graduate Employment Scheme (GES), but let us never forget a murky past which contained some of the more dubious aspects of the licensed teachers scheme. These included a back door route into teaching for individuals who had actually failed in, or had been counselled out from, courses of initial training. And who could ever forget the Mum's Army? Or the Articled Teachers Scheme – ditched mainly because it was too expensive, paying Articled Teachers, per year, the equivalent of half a student grant plus half an NQT salary. At the same time it lost credibility because it allowed some LEAs to manoeuvre candidates without appropriate entry qualifications, such as a recognised degree, on to a course through the 'back door'. These precursors of training schools were a significant distance away from attracting what the Green Paper (1998) describes as 'top quality teachers' through their GES. What the Government needs to be frightened of on behalf of the nation's schools is not the threat of an exclusivity of provision by higher education. What we should fear is the serious dropping of standards. The charges of protectionism, producer capture and monopolism are frequently smoke-screen charges levelled at higher education, when issues of standards are raised, which are inconvenient to those trying to spin the impression of innovation. Admittedly, people can be very pompous about standards and an appeal to standards is indeed often the last refuge of people resistant to change. Such charges cannot be fairly made against HE generally. Universities either as providers or validators, have committed themselves in recent years to all manner of 'alternative' programmes. They have worked with local schools and FE colleges on specific courses aimed to create access opportunities for ethnic minorities. From a basis of 'taster' courses they have created opportunities for graduates working in industry to cash in their past experience or qualifications and 'convert' that experience, or those qualifications, to become teachers in short time via part-time places or shortened degree courses – as little as $1\frac{1}{2}$ years, even. They have erected climbing frames for para–professionals such as nursery nurses to become nursery age teachers. Higher education has been proficient in the use of Assessment of Prior Learning (APL) and Assessment of Prior Experiential Learning (APEL) to the benefit of individuals and the profession. Moreover lest anyone argue that the Green Paper proposals for career-related modules for 'associate teachers' represent new thinking then they should check back on the evolution of diversified courses – the Dip HE was one specific example – in the post James Report 1970s. (The notion of payment though is certainly new!) What higher education has never done is sell the profession short on standards, and such a betrayal is the reality behind the notion of 'on-the-job training' which lies beneath some of the fine words. Certain of the proposals in the Green Paper, discussed above, if adopted in their crudest form, could potentially result in the destruction of both continuity and quality in teacher education.

We need only to look at the USA to receive an awful warning about what can happen when the dam is breached. A recently published book by some of America's most respected educational thinkers (Roth (ed.) 1999) vividly illustrates some of the pitfalls. A chapter entitled Grimm Tales by Raths makes a number of points in a moral tale of teacher education in the post war period and up to the present day. UK teacher educators and the DfEE could learn from his recommendations which are his conclusions after taking stock of the rapid recent growth of 'on-the-job training'. He would cancel entitlement agreements which provide a guarantee between successful programme completion and licence which he asserts are seriously flawed and undermine the autonomy of the university. He would also deny the right of states to approve teacher education programmes, which let them license teachers in terms of experience. He would use the National Council for Accreditation of Teacher Education (NCATE) (a body similar to England's CATE, the TTA's predecessor but one whose accreditation is sought and opted into) to establish a system whereby any graduates from accredited courses can seek employment in any state. He would further revise NCATE's standards to focus on process features such as quality, resources and evaluation practices, by contrast with England's content model. Clearly these recommendations mitigate against simple solutions to complex problems and promote policies that counter the erosion of standards and quality in teacher education programmes in the US. If implemented these points would deny the right of states to approve teacher education programmes idiosyncratically. This would avoid the resultant chaos which is emerging as 38 different States develop 'alternative' programmes, (Buck, 1995), and produce local licences and standards for teaching, or alternative certification programmes, some of which Clabaugh (1999) in the same book asserts are 'so undemanding they virtually ensure incompetence'.

It is surely a worthwhile aim that NCATE accredited teacher education units should allow candidates for teaching to apply successfully to *any* state in the US. Clearly size is important. It couldn't happen here it might be said. Oh really? With multiple providers? We should fear the spectre of highly localised certification, a potential existing in SCITTs, but still more likely in training schools cut off from partnership, and simply responding to supply issues influenced by a marketplace economy of teacher recruitment. Nightmare scenarios can be visualised. Clabaugh (1999) maintains that many of the US alternative certification programmes 'are just a way of putting warm bodies in front of classrooms'. He is highly critical of the way the Teach for America Programme (1992) is organised and lacks rigour – 'The plain fact is that no one can go from pedagogical ignorance to even entry level competence in just 30 class days of preparation!' (Clabaugh, 1999). He identifies the potential dangers of allowing big city school districts, the equivalent of a large LEA, to train their own teachers as like that of 'hiring a wolf as a sheep dog' and develops the analogy of the logic of the Teach for America initiative with 'Doctor for America'– a few weeks of summer training, some interning in an emergency room and more inner city experience – 'Over time they may learn from their mistakes, some might even become semi-competent'. Do elements of this risible scheme sound familiar? Paragraphs 111, 112, 117 and 130 of the Green Paper, Chapter Four would repay study.

Returning thus to England, one thought keeps recurring. How can the powers that be have it both ways? In one breath we hear that teachers and schools are failing their pupils, that existing teachers seriously need to update their professional knowledge especially in ICT, Literacy and Numeracy... and then in another breath that teachers in schools should be in the lead in teacher preparation in ICT, Literacy and Numeracy! If quality and standards are the order of the day then great care has to be taken with diversifying routes into teaching. Standards of entry requirements, content of courses or 'training' must be monitored closely across what could be an amazing number of providers, if schools should be categorised as individual providers. OFSTED's Teacher Education and Training Team could find itself to be unable to meet the demand and what then? Presumably a further call upon the superannuated or portfolio people whose shortcomings have too often been highlighted in their role as Additional Inspectors (AIs). The looming spectre is that of Quality (out of) Control.

It is not only the government which must have the vision to recognise that 'training schools' can logically only develop from established partnerships. Universities are proud of their partners, and they are particularly proud of those schools which have been in the vanguard of thinking about school-based training. However, they must now be prepared to 'let them go' to evolve to a different and higher status, taking over the role which has been traditionally that of university providers. This will not mean the end of university provision. Most schools will continue, as partners. This will be so not because those schools are not capable of becoming training schools. It will be because they will have chosen not to include such a role in their core purpose analyses. But, as argued above, there are others who see things differently, and, as teacher preparation environments, have come to maturity. It should be a familiar process to observers of those one time training colleges which became colleges of education but then left the University Area Training Organisations (ATO) to seek validation from the Council for National Academic Awards (CNAA). Many found themselves within Polytechnics to whom, as they grew, the CNAA granted increasing powers, finally cutting them free. It was then but a short journey to University status. It is probable that a 'training school' is an idea whose time has come. We should give much thought and effort to identifying those schools able and willing to take over the baton. Higher education will need to work with those schools in a different relationship. The product should be outstandingly successful, having grown naturally and organically out of partnership. Simplistic alternatives are likely to be cheap and nasty.

References

Bines, H. and Welton, J. (1995) *Managing Partnership in Teacher Training and Development*, London: Routledge.

Buck, G.H. (1995) 'Alternative Certification Programs: A national survey' *Teacher Education and Special Education* 18 (Winter), pp 39-48.

Campbell, A. and Kane, I. (1998) *School-Based Teacher Education: Telling Tales from a Fictional Primary School*, London: David Fulton

Clabaugh, A.K. (1999) 'Alternative or Just Easy?' in Roth, R.A. (ed.) *The Role of the University in the Preparation of Teachers*, London: Falmer.

DfEE (1998) *Teachers-Meeting the Challenge of Change* Green Paper, London: DfEE.

Downes, P. (1996) 'The Changing Balance in Initial Teacher Education' in Furlong, J. and Smith, R. *The Role of Higher Education in Initial Teacher Training*, London: Kogan Page.

Edwards, A. and Collison, J. (1996) *Mentoring and developing Practice in Primary Schools: Supporting Student Teacher Learning in School*, Milton Keynes: Open University Press.

McIntyre, D. and Hagger, H. (eds.) (1996) *Mentors in Schools : Developing the Profession of Teaching*, London, David Fulton.

Roth, R. A. (Ed.) (1999) *The Role of the University in the Preparation of Teachers*, London: Falmer.

Whiting, C., Whitty, G., Furlong, J., Miles, S. and Barton, L. (1996) *Partnership in Initial Teacher Education: A Topography*. MOTE Project, London, Institute of Education.

GREEN PAPER AND INDUCTION SUPPORT OR STRESS FOR THE NEWLY QUALIFIED TEACHER?

STEPHANIE PRESTAGE AND ANNE WILLIAMS

THE UNIVERSITY OF BIRMINGHAM AND KING ALFRED'S COLLEGE

Professional development starts when a new teacher first enters school. A statutory induction year will be introduced for those coming new to teaching from September 1999. The starting point for the induction will be the Career Entry Profile which identifies the strengths of each newly trained teacher and his or her priorities for further professional development. The Government will provide the necessary funding to guarantee all new teachers a reduced teaching load and a programme of support to ensure that they have the time to consolidate and improve their performance. (DfEE, 1998, p48)

Introduction

This paper uses the findings from a recently completed study of Newly Qualified Teacher (NQT) experience as the basis for consideration of some of the issues which the Government will need to resolve to achieve its stated aims. Our research focused upon the induction credit scheme feasibility study undertaken by the TTA in the 1997/8 academic year. The scheme involved 347 NQTs working in 185 schools, split fairly equally between the primary and the secondary sector. It encouraged the development and delivery of individualised programmes of induction and provided £500 per NQT to support this, together with a payment of £250 per school to support the monitoring and reporting. The project was co-ordinated through 36 lead bodies, including schools, Local Education Authorities (LEAs) and Higher Education Institutions (HEIs), each of which received up to £250 per participating school for co-ordination of feedback, interim and final report and attendance at meetings. The outcomes from this feasibility study were to be used to inform government decisions about the precise nature of the new induction arrangements. Our study, funded by the Association of Teachers and Lecturers, aimed to provide an independent evaluation of the NQT experience along with that of their mentors and to make recommendations which could inform future policy. Details of methodology and statistical analysis may be found in the full report of the project (Williams and Prestage, 1999). Here, we concentrate upon issues which emerged which are particularly relevant to the latest Government proposals.

The research project sought to:

- establish the range of induction/professional development activity or arrangements available to NQTs, including formal and informal, planned and ad hoc;

- establish the relative value of the different activities as perceived by NQT and mentor and the extent to which there is consensus;

- establish the relative value of the different activities as perceived by NQTs and mentors working in the primary and the secondary sector and the extent to which there is a shared view;

- investigate the conditions which enable specific activities to succeed;

- assess the extent to which the Career Entry Profile (CEP) (TTA, 1998a) has made an effective contribution to the NQT's development.

In order to achieve the above, we analysed both interim and final reports submitted by lead bodies, obtained information from NQTs and their mentors by questionnaire, and conducted a small number of follow-up interviews with NQTs and mentors.

Induction programmes

The induction of new entrants to the teaching profession has long been an issue (DES, 1992; GTC, 1992; OFSTED, 1993) and recognised as, at best, of patchy and inconsistent quality (HMI, 1988; Carre, 1993; Earley, 1993; Sidgwick, Mahony and Hextall, 1993; Bolam *et al.*, 1995). This is despite several years of intent to develop more effective induction, including recommendations from HMI, conferences to share and disseminate good practice and the use by the DfEE of Grants for Education Support and Training (GEST) to provide targetted financial support for use by schools and LEAs. Current proposals are for new regulations which will include both entitlement to support and procedures for assessment in order that QTS can be confirmed at the end of the first year of teaching. The proposed framework put out to consultation by the DfEE, aims to clarify expectations of NQTs; guarantee support and guidance; provide sufficient time and space to reflect and develop; opportunities to share experiences with other teachers; and to learn from observing them (DfEE, 1998a). The stated aim was that all NQTs should have structured support and training to consolidate and extend the skills learnt in their initial training. This would be done by building upon the best of current practice and establishing clear expectations of NQTs, together with a guarantee of the support and guidance needed to meet them (DfEE, 1998a). While a requirement that all NQTs should enjoy the benefits of high quality induction has widespread support, there is less certainty that this will be achieved through prescriptive expectations either of the induction and training components or of additional standards which need to be met by all NQTs for confirmation of QTS. The proposed arrangements published some months later by the TTA (TTA, 1998b) continue to include NQT support as an expectation, but give much greater attention to the assessment of the NQT. Despite an acknowledgement that few NQTs are likely to fail the induction year, the main focus of the document appears to ensure that the weak are removed at the expense of detailed consideration of strategies to ensure that the capable are supported.

Needs assessment

There are some fundamental questions about the needs of NQTs which require separation of needs as part of the process of moving from student to fully fledged teacher from particular professional development needs. The former might include resources such as additional non-contact time for preparation, or reduced additional responsibilities such as relief from pastoral duties. Also included might be a supportive environment, given the challenging nature of the first year in teaching. It could be argued that if these needs are not met then the likelihood of further development would be reduced irrespective of resources allocated to specific and targeted professional development activity. The Green Paper 'guarantees' funding for a reduced workload though, at the time of writing, it is unclear how LEAs and schools will receive this.

Both the Government and the TTA set great store by the Career Entry Profile (CEP) as a starting point for professional development. There is no doubt that the CEP has considerable potential and value, but there a several issues which remain to be resolved if it is to maximise its potential. First, the relevance of priorities identified by the NQT prior to taking up their post is doubtful. As an indicator of the NQT's performance as a student, they can provide a useful starting point for discussion, but many of our sample pointed to the speed with which they were overtaken by events, even when the NQT was employed in a school similar to that where they had spent their final teaching practice. Where the NQT obtained employment in a different kind of school, the targets identified at the end of initial teacher training are likely to be completely irrelevant in the new context. Indeed what was a strength in one context can easily become an area for urgent development in another.

Related to the CEP is the whole issue of target setting. This is another training issue, many of our sample noting that both NQTs and mentors found it difficult to set high quality targets. Target setting attracted more negative responses in the questionnaire than almost any other induction activity. Only 4 secondary NQTs found either short term or long term target setting using the CEP very useful and more than a quarter said that neither was useful. More secondary mentors questioned the value of target setting than of any other activity. An emerging theme was that the CEP was more useful in the second half of the year once the NQT felt settled in the new school context. Clearly the purpose and use of the CEP needs further evaluation.

Mentoring

Both the TTA scheme which we evaluated, and the DfEE consultation include access to mentoring by more experienced colleagues as central features of good induction. The problem is that there is little evidence that this happens currently (HMI, 1991; Edwards and Collison; 1996, Maynard, 1997; Moyles *et al.,* 1998). It appears that formal and informal mentoring decline over time for both students and NQTs; that the NQT was more likely than the student to be left alone once they were perceived to be 'doing OK'; that mentors cease to support students once they become autonomous; there is little evidence of mentors encouraging critical thinking. Where higher quality mentoring practice has developed, it has tended to be in the context of stable initial teacher training partnerships, as mentors gain experience over several years of working with students (Tomlinson, 1995). There are questions about how far this could be replicated in the induction context. These issues are likely to impact differently on primary and secondary schools. For many secondary schools, the employment of NQTs will be an annual, or almost annual, event. For primary schools, especially small schools, NQTs may only be employed very infrequently. The cost-effectiveness of training staff as mentors or in related areas of staff development is likely to vary significantly between the two phases. Moreover the need for particular mentoring skills may well be determined by factors such as school size. Nevertheless, a key theme emerging from all parties and at all stages of our current research is the centrality of high quality mentoring in any good quality induction programme, whether this be provided through highly organised structures or through embedding in the day to day practice of the school. The lack of reference to training for mentors or induction tutors, other than training in rigorous assessment, in the latest TTA consultation, is a serious cause for concern.

The variability in practice, both in levels of induction activity and in quality, raises serious issues about the likely success of this laudable initiative by the DfEE, in the absence of clearly identified and targetted funding to train staff in the mentoring of NQTs in the support and development area in addition to training in assessment. While observation of the NQT by a mentor was a feature of all participating in the feasibility study, several NQTs noted that observations were infrequent, sometimes very brief and often lacking in constructive follow-up. Both mentors and NQTs saw this partly as a resourcing issue and partly as a training issue as did a number of lead bodies. There were a number of comments in all phases of our study to the effect that the success or otherwise of NQT support and development depended entirely upon the quality of the mentoring available in the school. Schools with well developed initial teacher training partnerships with local HEIs were better placed than others to offer good quality mentoring. Given the expertise in mentor training and support which now resides in many HEIs, it is unfortunate that there is no acknowledgement in either the Green Paper or in the TTA consultation, of the contribution which HEIs could make to the preparation of mentors or induction tutors.

Funding

The issue of funding for induction was beyond the scope of our evaluation. However there is some anecdotal evidence from some consortia in the TTA scheme which underlines the need for this matter to be taken very seriously. It is particularly important to identify the additional costs which some schools have borne, because of the significant differences in the financial circumstances which pertain in different schools. While generalisations should be treated with caution, it is probably fair to say that secondary schools, because of overall budget size and staffing structures, are likely to be better placed than primary schools, to supplement centrally provided induction funding from their own resources both human and financial. Nias *et al.* (1989) note that limitations in resourcing in relatively small organisations, namely primary schools, can render them unable to make changes although they are not necessarily resistant to them.

The variations in levels of observation activity are one consequence of inadequate resourcing. Many schools commented on the need for resourcing to free the mentor in order for the role to be discharged effectively. This is particularly critical in the small primary school, with a teaching head. The resource issue also affected access to other opportunities. For example, those NQTs who had been able to visit other schools had invariably found this valuable, and a number identified this as the one activity which they would have liked to access. Yet few schools had been able to provide this opportunity because of the costs involved. Welcome though the Government commitment is to reduced teaching loads and programmes of support for NQTs, we wonder whether the financial support available will match the expectations. Those of our sample who offered information about resources suggested that the cost of high quality induction was between £2000 and £4000 per NQT, a costing which took no account of reduced workload.

Conclusion

All of the above points suggest that context is a key determinant of NQT need and of the likelihood of needs being met. The Green Paper and the TTA's proposals for the new induction arrangements assume that mandatory policy will bring about the desired improvement in practice. We believe that public policy is mediated in practice by the interpretations and meanings which are typically constructed by those on whom the policy impacts, in this case, NQTs, their mentors, headteachers and other induction providers (LEAs, HEIs, consultants). In addition to the mediating effect of the individual, the organisational culture of the school also affects teacher progress (Nias *et al.*, 1989; Carre, 1993; Lave, 1996). This culture may influence both the capacity and the willingness of those within it to engage fully with changed expectations with respect to the induction of NQTs.

Induction processes will impact differently upon, and be interpreted differently by, individual NQTs because each will bring their own prior knowledge, experience and beliefs to their first post. As a key person shaping the NQT's experience, mentor's beliefs, values and attitudes will also have a profound affect upon the nature of the NQT's induction year (Millwater and Yarrow, 1997). The NQTs in our sample had experienced very different introductions to teaching, many of which were related to school cultures, and none of which would be totally resolved by regulation or legislation.

We have only been able to address some of the issues which emerged from our work here. Our belief that NQTs deserve high quality support during their induction year was shared by all involved in the feasibility study, which probably represents better than average practice and, certainly, a high level of commitment by all involved. Even in these highly favourable circumstances, NQTs, mentors and lead bodies identified a number of serious issues which needed to be addressed, some of which have been discussed here. Few of these seem to receive sufficient attention in the latest proposals. We believe that NQTs deserve better than this, and that if the best are to stay in the profession and to develop further, some of these issues must be addressed. This is just as important as ensuring that the unsuitable do not remain in teaching.

The writers would like to acknowledge the financial support for the work reported here, provided by the Association of Teachers and Lecturers.

References

Bolam, R., Clark, J., Jones, K., Harper-Jones, G., Timtrell, T., Jones, R., Thorpe, R. (1995) The Induction of Newly Qualified Teachers in Schools: where next? *British Journal of In-Service Education*, 21, 3, 247-260.

Carre, C. (1993) The First Year of Teaching, in Bennett, N. and Carre, C. (eds) *Learning to Teach*, London: Routledge.

DES (1992) *Induction of newly-qualified teachers*, Administrative Memorandum 2/92.

DfEE (1998)*Teachers: meeting the challenge of change*, Cm4164, London: DfEE.

DfEE (1998a) *Induction for New Teachers: a consultation document*, London: DfEE.

Earley, P. (1993) 'Initiation Rights? Beginning Teachers' Professional Development and the Objectives of Induction Training', *British Journal of In-service Education*, 19,3, 5-11.

Edwards, A. and Collison, J. (1996) *Mentoring and Developing Practice in Primary Schools*, Buckingham: Open University Press.

GTC (1992) *The Induction of Newly Appointed Teachers: Recommendations for Good Practice*, GTC, England and Wales: NFER.

Great Britain, National Committee of Inquiry into Higher Education (1997) *Higher Education in the Learning Society, The National Committee of Inquiry Report 10-11, Teacher Education and Training, The Development of a Framework.*

HMI (1988) *The New Teacher in School*, London: HMSO.

OFSTED (1993) *The New Teacher in School*, London: HMSO.

HMI (1991) *School based Initial Teacher Training in England and Wales*, London: HMSO.

HMI (1992) *The induction and probation of new teachers: a report by HMI*, London: DES.

Hutchinson, D. (1994) 'Competence-based profiles for ITT and Induction: the place of reflection', *British Journal of In-Service Education*, 20, 3, 303-312.

Jaworski, B. (1994) *Investigating mathematics teaching: a constructivist enquiry*, London: Falmer Press.

Lave, J. (1996) 'The practice of learning', in Chaiklan, S. and Lave, J. (eds) *Understanding practice: perspectives on activitiy and context*, Cambridge: Cambridge University Press.

Mahony, P. (1996) 'Competences and the first year of teaching', in Hustler, D. and McIntyre, D., *Developing Competent Teachers: approaches to professional competence in teacher education*, London: David Fulton.

Maynard, T. (1997) *An Introduction to Primary Mentoring,* London: Cassell.

Millwater, J. and Yarrow, A. (1997) 'The mentoring mindset: a constructivist perspective?' *Mentoring and Tutoring*, 5, 1, 14-24.

Moyles, J., Suschitzky, W. and Chapman, L. (1998) 'Teaching Fledglings to Fly...?' *Mentoring and Support Systems in Primary Schools*, London: Association of Teachers and Lecturers.

Nias, J., Southworth, G. and Yeomans, R. (1989) *Staff relationships in the primary school*, London: Cassell.

Rabbett, P. (1998) *Interim findings on monitoring and support activities for Newly Qualified Teachers in the Induction Credit Feasibility Study*, London: TTA.

Simco, N. (1995) Professional profiling and development in the induction year, *British Journal of in-service Education*, 21,3,261-272.

TTA (1998a) *Career Entry Profile for Newly Qualified Teachers,* London: TTA.

TTA (1998b) *Induction for Newly Qualified Teachers: recommendations on monitoring, support and assessment arrangements, a consultation document*, London: TTA.

Tomlinson, P. (1995) *Understanding Mentoring* Buckingham: Open University Press.

Von Glaserfield, E. (1987) *Radical Constructivism: a way of knowing and learning*, London: Falmer.

Williams, E.A. and Prestage, S.A. (in press) *Still in at the deep end – developing strategies for the induction of new teachers, report of a study based on the TTA Induction Credit Feasibility Study*, London: Association of Teachers and Lecturers.

THE GREEN PAPER – COLOUR BLIND OR VISIONARY?

IAN MENTER

UNIVERSITY OF NORTH LONDON

Introduction

This Green Paper is a curious document. It is billed as a major, radical and ambitious review of teachers and teaching. The Prime Minister presents it as a modernisation programme ('the status quo is not an option'), the Secretary of State suggests it represents 'an opportunity to change the profession's pay and rewards for the better'. There are actually four substantive chapters, covering respectively: pay and rewards; leadership; training; support for teachers. Perhaps it is not surprising therefore that this hotchpotch should be something of a curate's egg, that is, good in parts.

It has been suggested that the debate around this document is likely to be the biggest opportunity to play a part in the discussion of the nature of teaching for a generation[1] and yet the creation of the General Teaching Council hardly warrants a mention (it is described in a half page box, DfEE, 1998a, p49). Many in the profession had seen the creation of the GTC as a major development in raising the status and professional standing of teachers, which in turn would bring about an improvement in recruitment. The document has been produced at a time of growing concern over the image of the profession and an emerging crisis of supply, perhaps greater than has been seen for many years.

The consultation is being conducted over a reasonable timescale of more than three months; however it is not clear what impact, if any, responses elicited through the consultation will have on subsequent policy. It is clear that the Green Paper will not lead to a White Paper and thence to a

..liamentary Bill. It seems fairly certain that some of the proposals are .1ot really likely to change in anything other than detail. Certainly there will not be any significant shift in the ways in which the 'challenges of change' are defined.

The focus of this chapter is very much on the underlying assumptions of this document. My purpose is to examine the Paper from an anti-racist perspective. That is, I am seeking to explore the extent to which the Green Paper may provide opportunities to develop an education service which recognises and responds positively to the multi-ethnic, multilingual, multi-cultural society in which we all live and the extent to which it identifies racism as a damaging force within education.

What emerges from this consideration is a conclusion that rather than being farsighted, as claimed, the Green Paper actually lacks imagination – it demonstrates no vision of the genuine connection between the work of teachers and social and cultural development. There is no recognition of the plurality of England and Wales, no recognition of the significance of Britain's place in Europe and no acknowledgement of the connections between our education service and the global society and economy.

I commence by looking at the 'vision' of society which the document portrays before discussing the approach taken to equal opportunities. I then consider questions of recruitment and professional development before looking in more detail at the chapter on training. In concluding I do offer some suggestions about alternative ways forward.

Vision of society

> *The Government wants a world-class education service for all our children. Every pupil should become literate, numerate, well-informed, confident, capable of learning throughout life and able to play an active part in the workforce and the community. All pupils should have the opportunity to become creative, innovative and capable of leadership. Pupils will need education for a world of rapid change in which both flexible attitudes and enduring values have a part to play.*
> (DfEE, 1998a, para. 1)

Few would find anything to argue with in this paragraph, other than perhaps seeking a definition of 'world class education service'. We may

46

agree that every pupil should develop the skills and have the opportunities which are listed. The simple fact is that other than emphasising that teachers should concentrate on numeracy, literacy and ICT, there is no attention given elsewhere in the document to the question of how teachers might develop other attributes in their pupils: confidence, learning capability, workforce and community activity. Nor is any attention given to opportunities for creativity, innovation or leadership. And in any case this statement is not enough – key skills in modern living include inter-cultural communication and decision making in a plural society. The final sentence of the above paragraph provides another tantalising phrase – 'flexible attitudes and enduring values'– should all attitudes be flexible and what are the enduring values which the government is promoting? If the Paper was based on an acknowledgement of the society we live in as diverse, dynamic and in need of change, one might expect to see some reference to pluralism, multilingualism, citizenship, personal, social and health education.

For a major policy statement emerging from the government a year before the 21st century it would seem reasonable to expect a much more forward looking approach. Where is the international dimension? For example, given the emphasis on electronic communications at several points in the document, it is surely regrettable that the opportunities which new technologies create for the development of global citizenship are not promoted. There is nothing in the document to indicate that England and Wales is anything other than an isolated homogeneous society whose only relationship with the rest of the world is one of competition. This is in spite of the fact that the Green Paper was published less than three months after the publication of a major report on 'Education for citizenship and the teaching of democracy in schools' produced by a committee established by the government and chaired by Bernard Crick (Advisory Group on Citizenship, 1998). Even this report seems strangely reluctant to focus on the nature and effects of racism, but it does certainly present our society as a fundamentally plural one. More recently, indeed subsequent to the publication of the Green Paper, we have seen two more documents from official sources – an OFSTED report on the achievement of minority ethnic pupils (OFSTED, 1999) and the McPherson report on the Stephen Lawrence case (McPherson, 1999) – which demonstrate a much clearer view of our plural society and the responsibilities of teachers in such a society. It is gaps between documents such as these and the Green Paper that really call into question the government's ability to offer 'joined-up policy'.

Awareness of equality of opportunity

An enormous amount of good work has gone on in the education service over many years – often against the odds – to raise standards and to open up equality of opportunity for all children. We need to go further. This means continuing to raise standards for all; it also means encouraging learning to high levels among those who, even in the recent past, have left school with little or no benefit from eleven years of compulsory education. (DfEE, 1998a, para. 2)

Much of the document deals with a new approach to the rewards to teachers, with proposals for fast tracking and linking pay to annual appraisal. One would expect a government which is committed to equality of opportunity to be signalling the importance of monitoring procedures designed to ascertain whether the achievement of promotion and increased remuneration is spread evenly by gender, ethnicity and able-bodiedness. Nowhere is there any reference to the possibility of unfair outcomes to such new practices.

What emerges is what used to be called a 'colour blind' approach. It is all very well talking about all children, but unless there is explicit acknowledgement of existing inequalities, whether by ethnicity, gender, special educational needs or whatever, a phrase such as this remains vacuous. It becomes the rhetoric of 'social inclusion' which we know is one of the key themes of government policy, without action to follow. Indeed it can lead all too easily to an approach which both stereotypes through labels such as 'urban disadvantage' and creates stigma through targeting 'failing schools' or 'failing teachers'. Gillborn (1999) has talked about the 'new racism' of 'New Labour' which seems entirely consistent with the non-specific 'all inclusive' 'all English' (oh, and Welsh) approach of this document.

The view of the document as 'colour blind' is reinforced when we come to consider questions of recruitment and career development in the next section.

Recruitment and career development

The Green Paper is published at a time of a growing recruitment crisis. There are longstanding shortages in some secondary subjects, notably physical sciences and mathematics. The shortages are far worse in some regions, particularly London, where there are also major difficulties in recruiting to senior posts in the early years and primary sectors as well as an emerging severe shortage of primary teachers in general. An appendix to the Green Paper outlines five short term measures being taken to boost recruitment. Its inclusion demonstrates the anxiety which exists in government about the current situation.

In the main part of the document, the section on recruitment makes no reference at all to the under-representation of members of minority ethnic groups in the current teaching profession, nor to their relative over-representation in the Section 11 workforce[2], compared with the mainstream. This is curious when there is an explicit reference to the under representation of men among those entering primary teaching in 1996-97 (14%, see para. 16).

Indeed if one took the photographic images in the document as an indication of the current workforce we would have the impression of a relative over representation of minority ethnic group members. Out of the eleven adults (presumed to be teachers) shown in these pictures, it appears that 2 are white males, 3 are minority ethnic males, 5 are white females and 1 is minority ethnic female. Of course, this is by no means an accurate reflection of the demography of the workforce, indeed if the images were to do that, out of eleven we could at the most expect to see one who was a minority ethnic group member. Rather it would seem that this visual representation is an attempt by the producers of the document to portray positively members of minority ethnic groups as teachers; it is in other words an example of presentational spin, what might have been called tokenism in the 1980s. It is of course probably a good idea to present such positive images, however it does throw into sharp relief the invisibility of the issue in the text of the document.

The single reference to recruitment of teachers from minority ethnic groups comes in Chapter 4 on training, where reference is made to the Teacher Training Agency's request to all training providers 'to set targets for the numbers of ethnic minority and male trainees to whom they offer places.' (para. 112) This reference is preceded by a statement that:

> *Teaching must attract high quality candidates from every section of society, bringing strengths and qualities which ensure that teaching is a vibrant and diverse profession.* (DfEE, 1998a, para. 112)

The target setting emerged at a conference held in November 1998 with a request for targets to be returned by early January 1999, perhaps reflecting an interesting view of the seriousness with which such a task should be undertaken.

Since the autumn of 1997 the TTA has launched a range of initiatives specifically designed to increase recruitment from minority ethnic communities. Some of these are listed in a report which emerged from a series of seminars organised jointly with the Commission for Racial Equality (TTA/CRE, 1998). The CRE has been fairly heavily critical of the TTA of its work in this arena, as demonstrated by an interchange between the chief executives of the two organisations which was conducted on the pages of the *Times Educational Supplement* (commencing with Ghouri, 1998). The CRE attack on the TTA was consistent with the research based view emerging from a study of the origins and development of the TTA as a government agency (Mahony and Hextall, 1997).

If we look at the ideas in the paper about professional development, as with the matter of differential rewards, we might hope for some assurance that there would be continuous monitoring of the profile of teachers successfully achieving of the various sets of standards and rewards framework-monitoring by ethnicity. After all it is not just important to increase recruitment from minority ethnic communities, it is crucial that career development opportunities are fully accessible to such recruits.

The nature of training/the training curriculum

A whole chapter (4) is devoted to the topic of training. In this section I wish to consider what might have been offered in this chapter. As it reads, the clear and central emphasis is on training teachers for what can be called the basic skills – literacy, numeracy and ICT. We see no acknowledgement of the need for understanding by teachers of processes of teaching and learning or for understanding of social and cultural processes in and around schools and their communities. We see again the kind of universalism attached to the British Standard Teacher (see Graham, 1998). There is no reference to the intellectual (thinking and analytical) skills and moral responsibilities which are fundamental attributes of successful teaching. This is consistent with the steady erosion of anything other than technical skills and (National Curriculum) subject knowledge formally expected of teacher training or judged directly through OFSTED inspections. Nor is there reference to the research base for effective teaching (even in the narrow sense offered by the TTA). Given this range of omissions, it is perhaps not surprising therefore that neither is there any reference to the role of universities in the initial education of teachers.

This Green Paper and this chapter in particular, provided an opportunity to bring a broader conception of teaching into the frame. The continuing narrow emphases on literacy, numeracy and ICT obscure the need for teachers to be equipped to work with pupils in a variety of contexts and actually to support the development of the kind of citizens to which the government aspires (as demonstrated in para 1, see above). Certainly it is unlikely to be possible to support the emergence of creative, confident citizens without good skills in literacy numeracy and ICT, but this is not sufficient. However, citizens of this kind will need a much fuller education than is implied by these emphases. They will need an education which offers a profound interest in artistic endeavour and in literature and the humanities. It is also an education which enables emergent citizens to grapple with political, moral and economic dilemmas. This is not necessarily a call for a return to 'cross-curricular elements'. Rather it is a call for the reintroduction of these areas of activity and learning into the proper professional domain of teachers' training, education and development. These are indeed areas where teachers' own professionalism can come very much to the foreground. They are areas where the best teachers already stand out and which all teachers should be well grounded in.

It has been suggested that this Green Paper is at too high a level of generality to offer details of what practical implications may follow. Indeed it has been suggested that 'the devil is in the detail', meaning presumably that the really important decisions will be made as the government circulars or memoranda which follow from the Green Paper are drafted. It is sad to say that so far the devil has indeed been in the detail.

The most obvious example is the DfEE Circular which currently describes requirements for Initial Teacher Training, Circular 4/98 (DfEE, 1998b). In this document national curricula for the English, Science, Maths and ICT components of Initial Teacher Training are prescribed. Throughout these sections of the circular it is very difficult to see any acknowledgement of the need for a national curriculum to reflect and respond positively to cultural diversity. There are references to children who are not yet fluent in English, but there is no positive reference to the strengths and opportunities created by the multilingualism of contemporary English society. Furthermore, in the section of the document which sets out standards which trainees have to achieve in order to be awarded Qualified Teacher Status, the only explicit references to matters of equal opportunities are requirements that trainees should be conversant with legislation such as the Race Relations Act and the Sex Discrimination Act. While this is clearly sensible, it is surely much more important that students should have an understanding of the many and complex ways in which racism can intrude into educational processes and experiences.

Conclusion

While applauding the underlying explicit purpose of the Green Paper to modernise the teaching profession and raise the quality of teachers and teaching, the contents of the document seem strangely inappropriate to this task. Reading the Green Paper in conjunction with other policy initiatives, such as the manner in which Section 11 is being deconstructed, can only lead one to believe that there is a less than wholehearted commitment to overcoming the barriers to equality of opportunity, such as racism.

There does seem to be an increasing problem of a disjunction between the DfEE and the TTA (and OFSTED). In many respects, the TTA defers to the DfEE for its policy steer and then provides the detail (with the devil in it). However the detail will be influenced by the broad policy steers given from the government (the Department) itself. Thus if these steers do not emphasise the pursuit of racial justice and equality, it is perhaps not surprising that policies on the ground leave much to be desired. In the area of recruitment, it would be fair to say that the TTA now appears to be making more of the running than the DfEE. On the question of the nature of teaching it is difficult to identify any serious movement in the DfEE,

QCA, the TTA or OFSTED[3], in spite of the continuation of a ministerial advisory group on 'raising the achievement of minority ethnic pupils'. There appears to be an alarming stasis in all four organisations. One can only hope that the establishment of a General Teaching Council may bring about some shift in priorities. However, it may be that the introduction of yet another government initiated organisation into the education policy arena simply establishes yet more and deeper policy contradictions.

In the Green Paper, the government proclaims:

> *We will be accused of being visionary and excessively ambitious. We plead guilty. After the years of drift, vision and ambition are surely what is needed. ... We urge all those with an interest in the future of our education system to give this Green Paper the most careful considera-tion and to grasp the historic opportunity that now presents itself.* (DfEE, 1998a, para. 35)

It is at least disconcerting that if this is indeed an historic opportunity, no legislation will follow nor will the consultation lead to a revised version of the document. This Green Paper is not serious about changing the demographic profile of the teaching workforce, nor about addressing the need to change the definition of what it is to be an effective teacher in contemporary society.

So many opportunities have been missed in this essentially reactive attempt to fix some problems in the education system that it is difficult not to become depressed. It would be foolish of course to reject the professed commitment by the Secretary of State and the Prime Minister to raise the status and indeed the quality of teachers, but to approach it in this piecemeal way is very short-sighted. It may be too late to say this now, but what is really needed is a major enquiry and investigation into the nature of successful teaching, with an assessment of how teaching does need to change the better to support the development of a just and open society in which citizens can play a full part in national, European and global affairs.

The authors of this Green Paper are guilty of a lack of vision and ambition. If this really is an historic opportunity then we must press the government to accept a vision of a society that is culturally and linguistically plural, that has a commitment to social justice, through opposing racism and other forms of injustice. We must press the government to have the ambition to recruit a teaching workforce that is drawn from all of the communities in England and Wales and to train every single teacher both through their initial teacher education and through the professional development framework to be equipped to work in and for a just multi-ethnic, multilingual society.

Notes

1 This is a reference to an answer given by Anthea Millett, Chief Executive of the TTA, to a question raised at the Annual Review Meeting of the TTA, 18 January 1999.

2 At the time of writing many Section 11 teachers are uncertain about their future because of the dismantling of Section 11 funding from April 1999. Monies for providing specialist support for bilingual pupils will be devolved to schools from that date.

3 The 1999 OFSTED Report on the achievement of minority ethnic pupils (OFSTED, 1999) is the first OFSTED publication to tackle questions of racism and discrimination in education in a direct way. We may wait to see whether the schools' inspection framework will be amended to reflect this new found awareness.

References

Advisory Group on Citizenship (1998) *Education for citizenship and the teaching of democracy in schools*, London: Qualifications and Curriculum Authority.

DfEE (1998a) *Teachers: Meeting the Challenge of Change Green Paper*, Cm 4164, London: The Stationery Office, December 1998.

DfEE (1998b) *Teaching: High Status, High Standards, Requirements for Courses of Initial Teacher Training* (Circular Number 4/98), London: DfEE.

Ghouri, N. (1998) 'Race chief attacks training negligence', *Times Educational Supplement*, 3 July.

Gillborn, D. (1999) 'Race, nation and education: New Labour and the new racism' in Demaine, J. (ed.) *Education Policy and Contemporary Politics,* London: Macmillan.

Graham J. (1998) 'From New Right to New Deal: Nationalism, Globalisation and the Regulation of Teacher Professionalism', *Journal of Inservice Education*, vol. 24, no. 1, pp. 9-29.

Mahony, P. and Hextall, I. (1997) 'Sounds of silence: the social justice agenda of the Teacher Training Agency', *International Studies in Sociology of Education*, vol.7, no.2, 137-155.

McPherson, Sir William (1999) *The Stephen Lawrence Inquiry*, Cm 4262-1, London: The Stationery Office.

OFSTED (1999) *Raising the Attainment of Ethnic Minority Pupils – School and LEA Responses*, London: Ofsted.

Teacher Training Agency/Commission for Racial Equality (1998) *Teaching in Multi-Ethnic Britain*, London: TTA/CRE.

LEADERSHIP, MANAGEMENT AND THE CHALLENGE OF CHANGE

LES BELL

LIVERPOOL JOHN MOORES UNIVERSITY

The Green Paper, *Teachers Meeting the Challenge of Change* (DfEE, 1998) devotes an entire chapter to leadership in schools in the context of managing change. This chapter is prefaced by the statement that:

> *All schools need a leader who creates a sense of purpose and direction, sets high expectations of staff and pupils, focuses on teaching and learning, monitors performance and motivates staff to give of their best. The best heads are as good as the best leaders in any other sector, including business.* (DfEE, 1998, p22)

This statement provides an insight of startling clarity into the conceptualisation of leadership and management in schools which underpins the current Government's education policy. The statement does not contain anything that is new but it does locate the responsibility for school management firmly and almost exclusively with head teachers. Previous policy statements have made it clear that heads will receive much of the credit for the success of their school and responsibility for failure:

> *The leadership qualities and management skills of the headteacher are a major factor contributing to a school's performance. When a school is put into special measures, one of the factors leading to this decision is often poor leadership ... In many cases the headteacher leaves the school* (OFSTED, 1998, p4)

Furthermore:

> *The vision for learning set out in this White Paper will demand the highest qualities of leadership and management from headteachers.*

The quality of the heads can often make a difference between the success or failure of schools. Good heads can transform a school; poor heads can block progress and achievement ... We need to ensure that in future all those appointed as headteachers for the first time hold a professional qualification which demonstrates that they have the leadership skills necessary to motivate staff and pupils and to manage a school. (DfEE, 1997, p46)

Heads, therefore, are central to the government's strategy. In order to ensure that they are fit for this purpose and can meet the challenge of change, a new hurdle in the race for headship has already been introduced, the National Professional Qualification for Headship (NPQH) which, the Green Paper assures its readers, will now become mandatory. It will deliver training which is, 'fresh and relevant, practical and professional' (DfEE, 1998, p27). This is to ensure that neither schools nor their heads are allowed to stand still. The Green Paper further promises a leadership programme for serving heads in order to refresh their skills and give them new inspiration. Once they have been prepared and assessed as suitable, heads have to lead and manage their school's improvement by using pupil data to set targets for even better performance while being subject to inspection and performance review: The Green Paper notes that:

OFSTED findings imply that one in seven of our schools is not well led. This is too many ... Where a head is unable to provide satisfactory leadership then evidently action needs to be taken. If a school is clearly failing then powers exist to close the school and install new leadership. (DfEE, 1998, p29)

Thus, the management and leadership as embodied in the Green Paper strongly post-Fordian (Bottery, 1998). Policy making and implementation strategy is becoming increasing centralised. Specific criteria for success are determined by central policy makers while a variety of providers are encouraged to compete against those criteria. The agenda focuses on raising standards but the standards to be attained are determined centrally. The responsibility for achieving those standards is clearly defined. In schools it rests with the headteacher. Schools that are meeting the defined standards or are striving to improve will retain their autonomy. Those that are believed to be failing will lose their autonomy and their heads may lose their jobs.

Such an emphasis on the centrality of the role of the head has been characterised by Grace (1995) thus:

> *Many contemporary texts on educational management ... use a discourse of 'leadership', 'vision' and 'mission'. Bottery ... lists the characteristics of the educational leader as 'critical, transformative, visionary, educative, empowering, liberating, personally ethical, organisationally ethical, responsible'... The rhetoric of the qualities which headteachers ... should display ... is becoming part of the checklist culture of educational management studies. Bottery's listing of these qualities constitutes a description not only of the ideal school leader but also of a person who must be seriously considered for canonisation as an educational saint.* (Grace, 1995, p 156-7)

The almost inevitable outcome of this focus on the head as the centre of management expertise and the locus of leadership within schools is that perceptions of headship are located within an hierarchical view of school management in which the head is the solitary, heroic leader (Bolman and Deal, 1991) who personifies and exemplifies the totality of leadership skills and managerial competences. This is the myth of the hero-innovator reborn. Like most myths, it fails to recognise reality. The conceptualisation of both leadership and management in the Green Paper incorporates perceptions drawn from the world of business and fails to acknowledge the dilemmas of leadership and management to which Grace (1995) has drawn our attention.

Leadership and management in all schools are inextricably linked. At its most strategic, management involves formulating a vision for the school based on strongly held values about the aims and purposes of education and their application to specific institutions and translating this into action. Leadership involves the embodiment and articulation of this vision and its communication to others. The fundamental flaw in the conceptualisation of educational management that leads to the over emphasis on the role of the head, exemplified in the Green Paper, is that the analysis stops at this point. No concept of shared or distributed leadership or acknowledgment of professional commitment can be found here. It is the head who, alone, is required to create the vision, establish the purpose and direction, set standards and motivate staff. Yet, if the vision is to be achieved it must be shared, not imposed. All members of the school community must be involved in its creation. This process must be facilitated by but not be restricted to the head or even to the head and senior staff. The purpose and direction of any school must be built on foundations which rest on the values and aspirations of its stakeholders and on the professional capability of teachers. This cannot be achieved unless leadership is shared.

Just as the vision, the purpose and direction for a school must be derived from the overarching values and beliefs of members of the school community, so their realisation requires action at the organisational and operational levels within the school. If management at the strategic level involves translating the vision into broad aims and long term plans, then it is at the organisational level that the strategic view is converted into medium term objectives supported by the allocation of appropriate resources and the delegation of responsibility for decision-making, implementation, review and evaluation. Thus, management and leadership must be developed at this level. Senior and middle managers in schools need to be committed to the school's vision because they have shared in its formulation, not had it imposed on them or sold to them. They must also have the capacity to lead and manage delegated in such a way as to enable them to convert the vision into strategy and the strategy into actions over the medium term. This demands shared leadership not management rooted in hierarchy. Such shared leadership is a necessary condition for the sound management of schools and not, as the Green Paper implies, a factor which may or may not be associated with success.

In turn, the implementation of these medium terms plans requires them to be further sub-divided into the totality of the delegated tasks that have to be carried out. At the operational level, therefore, resources are utilised, tasks completed, activities co-ordinated and monitored. This is often the responsibility of the class or subject teacher who also must be involved in the sharing of leadership responsibility rather than be subjected to a command and control approach to management. Thus the three levels of management must work in harmony towards a common purpose. This will not happen if the vision is not shared by all members of the school community and if values are not largely communal. Each level of management depends on the other two. To emphasise one and ignore the others or to reduce the role heads of department and curriculum leaders to that of managing teaching and learning without having a wider role in defining, achieving and sustaining the vision for the school is fundamentally to misunderstand the nature of educational management.

Head teachers cannot manage schools alone nor can they carry the burden of motivating others to achieve objectives and complete tasks without significant support from colleagues. Nor can head teachers be expected to meet the challenge of change alone. Meeting this challenge requires heads and their staff to move towards more inclusive forms of management and leadership than those embodied in the Green Paper. As Sergiovanni has argued, the most effective way to meet the challenge of change in schools is to move away from burdening head teachers with the sole responsibility for managing change and relocate that responsibility with individual teachers as part of their professional responsibility to their pupils (Sergiovanni, 1996). This requires a fundamental shift in the approaches which are adopted to change in schools. The approach to the management of change embodied in the Green Paper, termed by Sergiovanni 'rules-based', relies on:

• mandating new directions and practices, then providing the training and supervision to ensure their implementation

• standardising and tightly connecting the work that teachers do by engineering curriculum, teaching, scheduling, assessment and other dimensions of the work flows in ways that script the behaviour of teachers

• standardising the outcomes that teachers are to achieve in such detail that they all wind up doing pretty much the same things in order to get to the same place (Sergiovanni, 1996, p166)

How distressingly familiar that all sounds! Here is the traditional hierarchical management model with its rule bound inflexibilities and emphasis on the separation of functions. Yet the Green Paper exhorts teachers to meet the challenge of change. Such an organisational model cannot respond to change. The educational world of the future, the immediate future, is one in which school leaders will be required to confront a series of questions, the answers to which may lead to a radical restructuring of the very nature of schools:

Can staff have different working hours and conditions? Can greater use be made of technology so that 'learning' takes place when teachers are not there? Will all children be attending for five days in ten years time? Will part of lessons be conducted at home using the computer? Will traditional libraries become information centres bringing all pupils the best all the time by using available technologies? (Davies, 1997, p21)

In an unpredictable world uncertainty is the only certainty, that change is always with us and that this must lead to a rethinking of the nature of schools. As Morgan (1993) reminds us, we are moving into an age not of organised organisations but of organisations based on the ability to facilitate, encourage and understand in which self-organisation will be the key. Work relationships must move towards being less hierarchical and more multi-functional and holistic based on a wider distribution of power within the organisation. All schools must develop whole school perspectives. These are too important to be left to a single person or even a small group. It will then be seen that there are many ways of getting things done, each of which may be equally legitimate and that co-operation, responsiveness, flexibility and partnership must replace existing inflexible structures. This demands a norms-based approach to change rooted in:

professional socialisation, purposing and shared values, and collegiality and natural interdependence. Norms-based approaches are conceptually more complex than rules-based approaches. But once they are understood, they do not require complex management systems for implementation in schools. This ... encourages teachers to practise in more complex ways. They are able to make decisions that are more responsive to the unique circumstances they face. (Sergiovanni, 1995, p167)

Such an approach to change embodies an alternative conceptualisation of management and leadership from that in the Green Paper. This is a collaborative process of looking for what is right by accepting the validity of a range of different perspectives. Meanings are constructed and developed through reasoning with others, through narratives, rather than analysis, which take place within inclusive and communal relationships, the foundation of which is a commonality of experiences not a defence of differences. Such connected knowledge and the processes inherent within it, provide a foundation on which flexible yet inclusive policy formulation based on different but shared values and perspectives can be developed. The emphasis will be on holistic policies which focus on integration rather than fragmentation, which recognise that the sum is greater than the parts and celebrate the imaginative and the experimental. Collective responsibility will replace individual responsibility. The hero leader will no longer be isolated but will be given opportunities for sharing and devolving authority and responsibility. The mode of discourse will shift from debate to a dialogue which focuses on finding out rather than knowing, on questions not answers, which proceeds through listening not criticising, sharing rather than winning and losing and exploring new possibilities not defending established positions. Such an approach to leadership and management will enable the challenge of change to be met.

Bibliography

Bolman, L.G. and Deal, T.E. (1991) *Reforming Organisations: artistry, choice and leadership* Jossey-Bass: San Francisco.

Bottery, M. (1998) 'Rowing the Boat' and 'Riding the Bicycle' – Metaphors for school management and policy on the late 1990s. Paper presented to the 3rd ESRC Seminar, '*Redefining Education Management*' Open University: Milton Keynes.

Davies, B. (1997) 'Rethinking the educational context: a reengineering approach' in Davies, B. and Ellison, L. (1997) *School Leadership for the 21st Century* Routledge: London pp 11-22.

DfEE (1997) *Excellence in Schools* The Stationery Office: London.

DfEE (1988) *Teachers: Meeting the challenge of change* The Stationery Office: London.

Grace, G. (1995) *School Leadership: Beyond Educational Management: An essay in Policy Scholarship* The Falmer Press: London.

Morgan (1993) *Imaginization: The Art of Creative Management* Sage: London.

OFSTED (1998) *Making Headway* The Stationery Office: London.

Sergiovanni, T.J. (1996) *Leadership for the School House: How is it different? Why is it important?* Jossey Bass: San Francisco.

NEW PROFESSIONALISM – NEW ACCOUNTABILITY?

JOHN TRUSHELL
UNIVERSITY OF EAST LONDON

'Old' Professionalism

The Green Paper – *Teachers: Meeting the Challenge of Change* (DfEE, 1998a) – calls for 'new professionalism among teachers' (*ibid.*, para.13), asserting that:

> *The time has long gone when isolated, unaccountable professionals made curriculum and pedagogical decisions alone, without reference to the outside world* (*ibid.*).

This assertion is consistent with the observation of Simkins (1992) that there seems to be consensus, within policy circles, that 'old' professional accountability – to peers who would make judgements on criteria of 'good practice' – was 'tantamount to a total absence of 'real' accountability' (*ibid*, para 7). Notwithstanding this consensus, such criteria had been applied throughout teachers' careers, from aspiring professionals – those having achieved the status of 'teacher qualified to be considered for a post'– who had to demonstrate professional potential at interview (Beattie, 1996, p.12-13) to headteachers who had to demonstrate that they were 'leading professionals' (Laws and Dennison, 1991, p.47) to retain credibility within the profession (Hughes, 1990, p.26).

However, while these criteria of 'good practice' remained relatively subjective and insular, professional accountability alone was considered 'insufficient to ensure that educational provision [responded] to the complex demands of a modern economy and society' (Simkins, *ibid*, para 7). Hence, in this context, the Green Paper emphasises the need for teachers

– as modern professionals – 'to accept accountability' (DfEE, *op. cit,* para. 13) but, presumably, an accountability distinct from 'old' professionalism.

'Old' Accountabilities

The period of professional accountability – that 'time long gone' – passed a decade ago with the Educational Reform Act (1988), legislation representative of the 'new paradigm' for education which, paradoxically, promotes:

> *greater decentralization of decision-making and more collaboration, but within the context of increased state power over what goes on in local schools* (Carlson and Apple, 1998, p.8).

The nub of the paradox is that headteachers are required to implement greater democracy within schools 'by a government that is telling them to do this in a hierarchical manner' (Bottery, 1989, p.141).

The decentralization of decision-making through local management 'political' reforms and budgetary 'economic' reforms (Simkins, *op. cit.,* p.5) – 'increasing pressures on [headteachers] to be cost effective, competitive and measurably efficient managers of their schools' (Webb and Vulliamy, 1996, p.312) – compelled headteachers to become 'chief executives' (Laws and Dennison, *op. cit.*) while the implementation of curricular and assessment 'technical' reforms (Simkins, *ibid.*) compelled teachers to become technicians (Ball, 1990, p.155). Recent research – in secondary schools (Evetts, 1994) and primary schools (Webb and Vulliamy, *op. cit.*) – suggests that headteachers have been compelled to develop 'top-down directive styles of management' – 'creating a gulf between headteachers and their staff' (*ibid,* p.313) – which emphasised managerial accountability involving judgements made on the criteria of effectiveness and efficiency (Simkins, *op. cit,* p.7). Such criteria would be applied to teachers' delivery of National Curriculum materials and execution of National Assessments.

Compliance with state directives – including those introducing local management and budgetary reforms, and implementing technical reforms – emphasised political accountability involving judgements by representatives of specific stakeholder groups – who may serve as school governors – on the criteria of policy conformance (Simkins, *ibid.*). Such accountability binds not only the headteacher to the school governors but also teachers to school governors, parents and the wider community, to whom teachers have to explain the managerial aspects of the headteachers' role (Webb and Vulliamy, 1996, p.309-310), the technical aspects of their own roles, and the implications of each new directive for pupils.

The ascendancy of managerial and political accountability – and the relative decline of professional accountability – correspond with realignments of influence and roles within education, but the creation of a quasi-market for education introduced the problematic role of 'consumer' or 'customer' and the constrained influence of market accountability involving choices made by 'consumers' or 'customers' on the criteria of competitive success (Simkins, *op. cit.*, p.7). Education is a quasi-market insofar as the state determines overall funding and budgets, owns or employs the means of production, determines the curriculum and assessment (see Thomas, 1996) and consumes pupils as product (see Bottery, 1989, p.131-132). Parental choice of school – exercised on behalf of pupils – operates merely as an allocative mechanism for budgets in this quasi-market (Thomas, *op. cit.*, p.33). Market accountability is determined by schools' comparative success in National Assessments – as indicators of successful delivery of the National Curriculum – and the choice of the state to continue or discontinue funding.

New Accountability

The Green Paper announces that the state is to offer incentives under the School Performance Award Scheme:

> *A targeted national fund... for the purpose of offering non-consolidated performance bonuses to staff... [which] would be distributed to the top percentage of schools according to a range of performance indicators* (DfEE, *op. cit.*, para. 92).

The distribution of funds would 'depend on the success of appraisal' (*ibid.*, para. 94) – of headteachers and teachers – in accordance with a 'performance management policy' for which schools would be accountable (*ibid.*, para. 97). The policy would provide procedures for the appraisal of both headteachers and teachers by their respective hierarchical superordinates:

- governors, a 'trained external adviser' (*ibid.*, para. 45) and the head-teacher should agree and assess annual targets for school improvement – for example, 'broader indicators of school success such as student attendance rates, employability of school leavers or measurable impact of expanded community links' (*ibid.*, para. 44) – against which the headteacher's performance would be assessed by the governors and the adviser; and

- the headteacher and teachers should set annual individual targets – involving classroom observation and taking pupil progress into account – for 'improvement and development over the next year' (*ibid.*, para.79), 'at least one of which should be directly linked to the school's pupil performance targets' (*ibid.*, para. 80).

Such appraisal targets and procedures – which should ensure compliance of personal goals with the organizational goals of the school – will accentuate the meritocratic and bureaucratic aspects of an hierarchical structure in which:

- *heads and senior managers should manage the performance of teachers on a day to day basis* (*ibid.*, para. 95);

- *heads and teachers... will manage teaching assistants on a day-to-day basis* (*ibid.*, para. 143); *and*

- *assistants will provide an important resource for teachers to use in their developing role as managers of learning* (*ibid.*).

Reduction of teaching assistants to a resource for use by teachers is consistent with the underlying technical rationality of management theory and practice which reduces participants to means (see eg. Ball, *op. cit.*, p.157). Ironically, technical rationality and predictable and standardised working practices seem inconsistent with demands of contemporary society (Edwards, 1997, p.163) – which has been affected by 'a series of novel experiments in the realms of industrial organization... as well as in political and social life' (Harvey, 1990, p.145) – which values innovativeness and flexibility (DfEE, *op. cit.*, para.1).

Yet, herein lies the nub of a second paradox: greater standardisation of pedagogy and assessment and greater centralization of decision-

making are justified as the means by which greater flexibility and innovativeness will be achieved (Wexler, 1998, p.179).

New Professionalism

These two paradoxes in education are not novel as Husòn (1979) observed:

On the one hand the school is expected to implement goals of a democratic and anti-authoritarian character; on the other hand it is, like private and public business, part of a huge bureaucracy, which is governed from the top down (ibid., p.125).

These tensions, Husòn contended, were consistent with the contradictory aims of education:

- an explicit aim of... individual self-realization ; and

- an implicit aim of producing citizens for the various slots in the labour market' (*ibid.*).

While Anglo-American-Australian states may maintain some pretence of facilitating self-realisation, education provision has been restructured to produce pupil-product for consumption by 'restructured, post-Fordist, post-industrial work' (Wexler, *op. cit.*) in which context 'flexibility' refers to transferable skills relevant to the workplace and 'innovativeness' refers to selective application of such skills in the workplace.

This restructuring of educational provision has had serious consequences for methods of instruction, evaluation of student progress and the way teacher and student role are played (Husòn, *op. cit.*, p.126). Reviewing the role of the teacher in the period of 'old' professional accountability, Husòn contended that the teacher had three technical roles:

- the organizer of learning opportunities for the individual student;

- the guide of the learning process; and

- the examiner of learning outcomes (*ibid.*, p.168).

However, technical reforms in the United Kingdom during the 1980s restricted those roles of the teacher as guide and examiner to that of executor of curriculum plans, pedagogical processes, and assessment procedures which had been determined centrally and standardised in a restructured education system. Moreover, pedagogical initiatives during the 1990s – such as the National Literacy Strategy (DfEE, 1998b) and the planned National Numeracy Strategy – will further restrict these roles.

The remaining role of the 'old' professional – that of organizer of learning opportunities for individual students – the Green Paper seeks to modernise, contending that:

> *Throughout this century teachers have had to choose between priori-tising the needs of large groups or following up the diverse needs of individuals. Now for the first time they can realistically do both* (DfEE, 1998a, para. 5).

Moreover, the Green Paper envisages that learning opportunities for individual students will be realised and mediated by the resource of class-room assistants with teachers as managers of learning (*ibid.*, para. 143), contending that, with assistants:

> *teachers can choose between large groups and small ones, assigning additional staff to provide extra assistance to those [pupils] with special educational need or to help push on the gifted* (*ibid.*, para.7).

However, these managed learning opportunities for individual students – whether extra assistance or push – will be constrained by those centrally determined and standardised curriculum plans, pedagogical processes, and assessment procedures.

While the 'old' professionals have been deskilled as guides and examiners, and will be reconstructed as managers rather than organizers of learning opportunities, contemporary teachers have been urged to believe that commitment to school development plans, school review and appraisal will achieve greater professionalism (Ball, *op. cit.*, p.162), or new profes-sionalism. The 'authority of expertise' (Bush, 1995, p.53) which 'old' pro-fessionals exercised as guides, examiners and organizers will be replaced by the 'positional authority' (*ibid.*) of the new professionals as middle-managers – poised between teaching assistants and headteachers – in a meritocratically, bureaucratically and hierarchically structured 'educa-tional corporatism' (Wexler, *op. cit.*, p.178).

The Green Paper simply states that recruitment of prospective teachers is challenged by:

> the present reality of teaching [which] too often compares unfavourably with the growing range of alternative careers for successful graduates (DfEE, 1998a, para.18).

Apparently, the simple solution posited by the Green Paper is meeting this challenge by changing teaching into an alternative managerial or executive corporate career which will attract successful graduates.

References

Ball, S. (1990) 'Management as moral technology' in Ball, S (ed.) *Foucault and Education* London: Routledge 153-166.

Beattie, N. (1996) 'Interview and concours: teacher appointment procedures in England and Wales and France, and what they mean' *Assessment in Education: Principle, Policy and Practice* vol.3 (1) 9-28.

Bottery, M. (1989) 'The education of business management' *Oxford Review of Education* vol.15 (2) 129-146.

Bush, T. (1995) *Theories of Educational Management* 2nd ed. London: Paul Chapman Publishing.

Carlson, D. and Apple, M.W. (1998) 'Introduction: critical education theory in unsettling times' in Carlson, D. and Apple, M.W. (eds.) *Power/Knowledge/Pedagogy* Bolder, Colorado: Westview Press 1-38.

Department for Education and Employment (DfEE) (1998a) *Teachers: Meeting the Challenge of Change* London: Department for Education and Employment.

Department for Education and Employement (DfEE) (1998b) *The National Literacy Strategy: Framework for Teaching* London: Department for Education and Employment.

Edwards, R. (1997) *Changing Places* London: Routledge.

Evetts, J. (1994) 'The new headteacher: the changing work culture of secondary headship' *School Organisation* vol.14 (1) 37- 47.

Harvey, D. (1990) *Condition of Postmodernity* Oxford: Blackwell.

Hughes, M. (1990) 'Educational administration: international trends and issues' *International Journal of Educational Management* vol.4 (1) 22-30.

Husòn, T. (1979) *The School in Question* Oxford: Oxford University Press.

Laws, J. and Dennison, W.F. (1991) 'The use of headteachers' time: leading professional or chief executive?' *Education 3-13* vol.19 (2) 47-57.

Simkins, T. (1992) 'Policy, accountability and management: perspectives on the implementation of reform' in Simkins, T. Ellison, E. and Garrett, V. (eds.) *Implementing Educational Reform: The Early Lessons* London: Longman 3-13.

Thomas, H. (1996) 'Efficiency, equity and exchange in education' *Educational Management and Administration* vol.24 (1) 31-47.

Webb, R. and Vulliamy, G. (1996) 'The changing role of the primary-school headteacher' *Educational Management and Administration* vol.24 (3) 301-315.

Wexler, P. (1998) 'Self and education: reversals and cycles' in Carlson, D. and Apple, M.W. (eds.) *Power/Knowledge/Pedagogy* Boulder, Colorado: Westview Press 174-190.

'FREEDOM TO MANAGE' LEADERSHIP, EXCELLENCE AND THE NEW PROFESSIONALISM

LOUISE MORLEY

UNIVERSITY OF LONDON INSTITUTE OF EDUCATION

Introduction

This chapter will examine the new professionalism advocated by New Labour (DfEE, 1998). It will consider how values, as well as technologies and drive systems from the cultural world of business and commerce have been imported into education, bringing with them new meanings, priorities and truths. In the Green Paper (DfEE, 1998) school effectiveness and academic achievement have been discursively linked to leadership qualities of headteachers. The effective school is thought to combine culture management (the creation of purposes and meanings) with performance management (measuring what is thought to matter). Whereas professionalism formally involved the critical deployment of discourse, it has shifted from understanding to performance. Performance is now an organisational responsibility, and implementation of macro value systems to the microprocesses of the organisation are mediated through leadership. Management responsibility is both delegated and monitored. Consistent with post-Fordist multiskilling, a new interface between management and professionalism has emerged, with headteachers constructed as both educators and systems engineers. New incentives, frameworks for professional education and reward systems are being introduced to reinforce dominant ideologies. This chapter will raise questions about whose interests are represented, as well as which systems work.

Modernising Education

The 1980s witnessed an intersection of political rationalities with manage-ment technologies. A new interface between management and profes-sionalism emerged. The grand narrative, or 'truth' of new managerialism as a transformative device was spoken by key politicians, such as Michael Heseltine, the Secretary of State for the Environment in 1980:

> *Efficient management is the key to the [national] revival... And the management ethos must run right through our national life – private and public companies, civil service, nationalised industries, local government, the National Health Service* (Heseltine, quoted in Pollitt, 1993, p.3).

Underpinning this statement was the requirement for the public services to earn their legitimacy and to demonstrate performance (Morley, 1997). There is a fundamental belief that objectives of social policy can be pro-moted at a lower cost when appropriate management techniques are applied to the public services. The indeterminacy of the social world can be regulated and controlled by effective management. Ball (1990) notes that the term 'management' is the linguistic antithesis to chaos, and implies rationality in the face of unruliness. The Green Paper is full of dichotomous images relating to old and new regimes. For example, 'After years of drift, vision and ambition are surely what is needed (para. 35).' Images of decay, under investment, and low status such as battered kettles in staffrooms and old photocopying machines contrast with the new ambience of modernisation and morale boosting rallying cries. Policy interventions are legitimated by associating the past with low educational standards and Dickensian working conditions.

The effectiveness movement initiated by the New Right created new institutional norms and patterns, and new logics of appropriateness (Morley and Rassool, 1999). These meanings have been continued within the New Labour educational policy framework. They have been re-articu-lated in terms of a stakeholder society, commitment to excellence and a passing concern with social inclusion and the spiral of disadvantage. With many of the systemic and structural changes following the 1988 ERA now in place, New Labour policy initiatives in education so far have shifted to the regulation of quality (DfEE, 1997). Quality and excellence have been discursively linked to management, leadership and a new professionalism in education. Ignoring etymology, Tony Blair writes in the Foreword of the Green Paper 'We need excellence to become the norm'. This normalised excellence is to be achieved via modernisation. Behind judgements of quality are judgements of value. However, there is a tacit notion of what constitutes excellence in the Green Paper with no indication of contestation or contradictory interests. Management has been naturalised and there is a continued commitment to making education more auditable, with reductive performance indicators as signifiers of progress and change. A central constituent of the modernisation process is to strengthen school leadership and offer rewards for higher standards, thus reinforcing the performance ethos.

Managing Standards

New managerialism in education has implied that the 3 Rs are best achieved via the 3 Es (economy, efficiency and effectiveness). Values, as well as technologies and drive systems from the cultural world of business and commerce have been imported into education, bringing with them new meanings, priorities and truths. The introduction of markets and managers has been a generic transformational device designed to restructure and re-orient public service provision. The common elements have involved site-based management, the language of improvement and budgetary devolution. New organisational forms are thought to hold the key to means-ends efficiency and quality assurance in education. Clarke and Newman (1997, p.ix) describe managerialism:

> as a cultural formation and a distinctive set of ideologies and practices which form one of the underpinnings of an emergent political settlement.

Central to new managerialism is the promotion of a corporate mission, with goals, targets, monitoring procedures and performance measurement. Responsibility is devolved and increased responsiveness to clients/customers is alleged. The creation of quasi markets and structural decentralisation has created a new power base from which managers can operate. There is an appearance of relative autonomy, such as LMS, but this is carefully screened by the gaze of authoritarian central controls. New managerialism represents the atomisation of control. Responsibility is dispersed and devolved so that every organisational member is burdened with income generation, quality, standards and performance. In the elision of teacher with manager, emphasis has shifted from job specification to performance specification. The failing school and low standards have been discursively constructed as risks to public interests. The new professionalism implies a considerable amount of risk management and risk reduction. There is a powerful mechanism of disciplining and self-disciplining. As Thrupp (1998) argues, regulatory organisations such as OFSTED gain their ideological power from holding school staff responsible for school effectiveness. There is a myth that increasing the workload for teachers results in enhanced effectiveness (Reay, 1998). While there appears to be a consensualist assumption regarding mission, targets, and commitment to quality and customer responsiveness, educators are faced with longer working hours, and disappearing job security. Campbell and Neill's survey on the effects of the National Curriculum on primary school teachers (1994) found 54 hour weeks were the norm, while there had been no overall improvement in standards. This raises questions about whether the pressure of performance is more linked to a desire for governmentability than effectiveness. These dilemmas are often reduced to the debate about whether educators have been deprofessionalised or, indeed, reprofessionalised. A key question is who benefits from this process and what are the costs?

Charismatic Change Agents Lead the Way

New managerialism has glamorised the manager. As Clarke and Newman (1997 p.36) humorously point out, the new image has transformed 'the bureaucratic time-server to dynamic leader'. The discursively reconstituted functionary is now a charismatic change agent and risk-taker, associated with innovation, corporate culture and enterprise. The headteacher's agency can overcome wider social structures of inequality. The headteacher has been reconstructed, or reprofessionalised as a manager. The enterprise culture has allowed public service managers the opportunity to demonstrate their connection to the business world, with pressures and incentives operating at a number of levels. The Green Paper (DfEE, 1998, p.21) states that:

Good heads are crucial to the success of schools. We need to develop strong leaders, reward them well and give them the freedom to manage, without losing accountability.

There is an interesting juxtaposition between 'freedom to manage' and 'accountability', suggesting prescribed parameters for leadership, reinforced by financial incentives. While accountability is an important aspect of democracy, signifiers of educational performance nevertheless have been reduced and schools have been forced into elaborate procedures for impression management (Ball, 1997).

The new Education Action Zones are dependent on partnerships between the public and private sectors. The rationale is both a holistic approach to urban regeneration, and a belief that schools have a lot to learn from private sector management techniques. In the juxtaposition of professionalism with managerialism, there has been a bureaucratisation of professionalism and a new compliance culture. Clarke and Newman (1997) mention there has been the creation of new subjects who enact the discourse of new managerialism. Corporate loyalty and organisational performance are cornerstones of new managerialism and school effectiveness, both in terms of advertising results, but also in the way that rituals are enacted regardless of their efficacy. So, schools produce action plans, mission statements, targets, strategies and visions as a matter of symbolic compliance or legitimation – that is, producing the symbols that schools are expected to have.

The reconstructed headteacher is a systems engineer and the system is driven by national assessment. There is a set of assumptions in the Green Paper about what constitutes effective leadership. Leadership is a controversial concept, often embedded within classic hierarchical thinking and polarised notions of the leaders and the led. However, in the Green Paper, it is represented as automatically benign and upbeat. Leaders are represented as uncontested figures 'who purport to restrict themselves to the realms of fact, means and measurable effectiveness' (Wilcox, 1997, p.252). The unproblematic construction of leadership and shared vision implies that organisational culture is based on consensus, rather than conflict (Ball, 1987; Morley, 1999). Power is left untheorised. Micropolitical processes in the school and the way in which power relations and competing interests interact with change programmes are ignored.

Reay (1998) highlights a further contradiction in so far as school effectiveness discourses give primacy to leadership skills and the role of the headteacher while simultaneously purporting to value team-building and collegiality. The recommendations for performance related pay in the Green Paper (DfEE, 1998), and the introduction of para-professionals, create a tiered teaching profession, with divisive organisational culture based on competition and individualism. These factors seriously impede collaboration and a team approach to change processes. However, new managerialism has reinforced the notion of corporatism. There is the belief that meanings, values and beliefs are shared, and that these are disconnected from issues of power, control and hierarchy. Equally, barriers to participation, such as gender, 'race', social class, sexual orientation and disability are left unexplored. The Green Paper (DfEE, 1998), like so many documents concerned with school effectiveness, addresses a universal subject, undifferentiated by gender, social class, ethnicity. It is assumed that the leader will intuitively understand what is in the best interests of the school, and will be able to represent the interests of others. The leader is thought to embody the most appropriate values and visions for everyone concerned. Complex educational issues are reduced to challenges for different management techniques and strategies. Angus (1994, p.85) notes how:

> ... it is believed that leaders of vision are able to bring about a negotiated order which accords with their own definitions and purposes and ensures that any change is directed into reasonable, predictable channels by their own overriding moral force. Other organisational participants, such as teachers, parents and students... are generally viewed as passive recipients of the leader's vision.

Headteachers are now viewed in much the same light as chief executives in industry, and are to be remunerated as such (DfEE, 1998). It is questionable as to whether this reconstruction has been resulted in deprofessionalisation or reprofessionalisation. Sinclair et al. (1993) argue that headteachers are no longer partners in the education of pupils, but have been reduced to the role of allocating resources, rewards and ensuring that the activities of employees are appropriate to the needs of business. In this analysis, the new professional is no longer associated with being in command of a body of knowledge. External drive systems now shape professional identity, rather than internal notions of reflexivity and reflection. There has been a significant shift from understanding and critical knowledge towards performance.

Summary

Political objectives have been achieved, in part, by the establishment of a managerial ethic in education, as in other public services. There has been an emergence of new organisational forms as well as the structural and systemic changes that have evolved in the UK economy during the 1980s, as important elements in the process of economic restructuring. Professional meaning and purpose have been framed by the performance culture. Performance is thought to be enhanced by accountability. There are few indications of the nature of educational development beyond concerns about performativity. A positivistic view of educational change and development relies predominantly on quantitative data as a basis for policy decision-making. At a deeper level, it engages schools in the totalising process of self-monitoring and self-correction. The concept of excellence in schools that now features in the New Labour educational policy framework consolidates the technical-rational approach that framed the market-orientation of Conservative education policy. Whereas traditionally, the challenge to professionals has been the handling of multiple and often contradictory discourses (Barnett, 1997), an ongoing occupational closure has emerged with a shift in emphasis from dialogical to bureaucratic processes. To articulate these concerns is to position oneself as Luddite in the face of the modernisation process. Within the new action-oriented Labour policy, critique and reflection are frequently oppositionally located to change and modernisation.

References

Angus, L., (1994) 'Sociological Analysis of Educational Management'. *British Journal of Sociology of Education*, 15 (1), 79-92.

Ball, S. J. (1987) *The Micropolitics of the School*. London: Routledge.

Ball, S. J. (1990) Management as Moral Technology: A Luddite Analysis. In Ball, S. J. (ed.), *Foucault and Education*, (pp. 153-166) London: Routledge.

Ball, S. J. (1997) Good School/Bad School: Paradox and Fabrication. *British Journal of Sociology of Education*. 18 (3), 317-336.

Barnett, R. (1997). *Higher Education: A Critical Business*. Buckingham: Open University.

Campbell, J., and Neill, S. (1994) *Curriculum at Key Stage 1: Teacher Commitment and Policy Failure*. Harlow: Longman.

Clarke, J. and Newman, J. (1997) *The Managerial State*, London: Sage.

Department for Education and Employment (DfEE) (1997) *Excellence in Schools*. White Paper presented to Parliament by the Secretary of State for Education and Employment by Command of Her Majesty, July 1997, London: HMSO.

Department for Education and Employment (DfEE) (1998) *Teachers Meeting the Challenge of Change* (Green Paper). London: HMSO.

Morley, L. (1997) Change and Equity in Higher Education, *British Journal of Sociology of Education*, 18 (2), 231-242.

Morley, L. (1999) *Organising Feminisms: The Micropolitics of the Academy*, London: Macmillan.

Morley, L. and Rassool, N. (1999) *School Effectiveness: Fracturing the Discourse*. London: Falmer Press.

Pollitt, C., 1993, *Managerialism and the Public Services: Cuts or Cultural Change in the 1990s* (2nd edition), Oxford: Blackwell.

Reay, D. (1998) 'Micro-politics in the 1990s: staff relationships in secondary schooling', *Journal of Education Policy*, 13(2), 179-196.

Sinclair, J., Ironside, M., Seifert, R. (1993). Classroom Struggle? Market Oriented Education Reforms and Their Impact on Teachers' Professional Autonomy, Labour Intensification and Resistance. International Labour Process Conference, 1 April. .

Thrupp, M. (1998) 'The art of the possible: organizing and managing high and low socio economic schools', *Journal of Education Policy*, 13 (2), 197-219.

Wilcox, B. (1997) 'Schooling, School Improvement and the Relevance of Alasdair MacIntyre', *Cambridge Journal of Education,* 27(2), 249-260.

REGULATING THE CHAOS
THE IRRATIONALITIES OF TECHNICAL CONTROL IN TEACHER EDUCATION

NAZ RASSOOL

UNIVERSITY OF READING

Introduction

Raising standards in education, maximising teacher performativity, effective leadership and continuous improvement provide the basis of the New Labour Government's vision of a 'world class' education system for England and Wales in the Third Millennium. This chapter argues that far from being visionary, the principles of modernisation underscored in the Green Paper, *Teachers – Meeting the Challenge of Change* (DfEE, 1998), present a myopic view of social change – and the role of teachers and education within this process. It explores the extent to which the Green Paper as a discursive process consolidates the putting into place of rigid systems, structures, and practices aimed at providing universalistic solutions to multifaceted problems within a highly differentiated education system. It suggests that this technical – rational approach to educational change and development lacks the scope to accommodate the complex skills and knowledge demands of a dynamically changing global cultural economy.

Educational Policy and Economic Restructuring

The centrality of educational reform to the New Labour political project gives an indication of the high level of priority accorded to the restructuring of the educational system. Represented as 'modern' policies to suit a 'modern' economy within a 'modernising' social milieu, educational policy initiatives during the past two decades have played an important role in the state's management of hegemonic relations during a sustained period of social transition. Central to the 'modernisation' project is the need to bring education in line with changing economic realities within a highly competitive global economy. Driven, at least in part, by technological development and changing markets, the imperative to increase worker efficiency, cost-effective production, innovation and enterprise have provided the economic rationale for the complete overhaul of the educational system. Focused on 'real world' concerns, school effectiveness policy interventions thus are seen as offering concrete solutions to both long- and short-term educational, economic and social problems. The precision and quantifiable measurement reflected in school effectiveness taxonomies and procedures, are seen to inject levels of certainty into a world in a constant state of flux. Thus they serve to provide hegemonic support to the new (emerging) regime of accumulation. Within the framework of French regulation theory, the term 'regime of accumulation' refers to 'the specific institutional framework and social norms proper to various stages of capitalist development' (De Vroey, 1984, p.52). The establishment of new social 'norms' refer to not only the re-composition of the labour force, the restructuring of the labour process and commodity relations, but also a reshaping of worker consciousness. In restructuring the education system as a whole, neo-liberal – and now New Labour – policy meanings have served to redefine not only the educational process but also teachers' consciousness as workers, and the expectations and role of parents as consumers. Viewed within this context, the structural and systemic changes within education can be seen as forming an important part of the new (emerging) mode of capitalist regulation. These meanings are consolidated in the Green Paper, *Teachers – Meeting the Challenge for Change* (1998, p.11; henceforth referred to as the Green Paper). Building on key themes in the prevailing school effectiveness discourse, the Green Paper aims to put into place a modern professionalised education system as an integral part of a modernising state.

Towards a Technocratic Modernisation

Modernisation within the New Labour ideological framework represents an eclectic set of values. It subscribes to the notion of the risk society (Beck, 1992) with its inherent dynamic for conflict and catastrophe on the one hand, and its rich potential for innovation and change on the other.

Within this framework, concepts of social justice and equity sit contradictorily alongside rational self-management and corporate business values. In seeking to deal with the uncertainties that predominate in modern life, it is said that people increasingly place their trust in 'expert-systems' as an essential part of a reflexive 'life planning' (Giddens, 1991, p.147). Expert-systems are seen to comprise technical or professional expertise that organise large areas of the social and material environments that we inhabit in the modern world (Giddens, 1991). To ensure high-reliability, expert-systems are subject to regulation as a means of protecting consumers. Thus they are seen as representing rational frameworks to support self-management amidst the chaos of everyday life in the contemporary world. For Giddens (1991; 1998) the concept of self-management forms an integral part of institutional reflexivity that is grounded in a process of self-definition and self-identification. Success depends on the self-help and self-managing strategies adopted; it becomes a discerning 'life-style' choice. The problem with this view is that it assumes a unified subject in dialogue with a cohesive and homogeneous social world. It leaves discursive forms of power and, especially, different forms of oppression within the modern world largely unaddressed.

Transferred to education, the ideology of the risk society translates schools into 'expert-systems' requiring high levels of teacher professionalism. This professionalism is defined in terms of teachers:

- having high expectations,

- accepting accountability,

- taking 'responsibility for improving their skills and subject knowledge',

- seeking 'to base decisions on evidence of what works in schools in this country and internationally',

- working co-operatively as members of a team and with outside interests, and 'to anticipate change and promote innovation' (DfEE, 1998, p.14).

Here professionalism is defined in terms of teachers having positive attitudes to change, worker and skills flexibility, the motivation to work, the ability to adapt rapidly to change, and rational self-management. The onus for employment is transferred to individual teachers and their suitability according to a circumscribed set of performance criteria. These in turn are defined largely in terms of functional skills, self-monitoring and self-regulation aimed ultimately at avoiding systems failure.

Failing schools and failing teachers are perceived as risks to the public, in much the same way as faulty engines on an aircraft. There is now increasing emphasis on developing schools as high reliability organisations with zero-defects in the products, procedures and processes (Reynolds, 1996; DfEE, 1997; DfEE, 1998; Slee, 1998). In line with Japanese production strategies, the overall emphasis is on *process* in which concerns or problems are evaluated in terms of worker discipline, time management, skill development, participation and involvement, morale and adequate information flows (Morley and Rassool, 1999). Emphasis is placed on capacity-building through effective leadership, the ability of teachers to recognise 'blocks' in the process of change, the need to have the capability to identify the means to overcome these and to self-correct and/or to map out the scope of change. Through this 'on-task' process teachers as functional workers are incorporated conceptually, psychologically and physically into the culture of the work place, and further subjected to the totalising 'gaze' of task, self- and external monitoring.

Hallmarking Education

Whereas the overall emphasis in Conservative policy in education was on marketisation, New Labour's educational project foregrounds the principles of *quality* and *excellence* in schools. These concepts represent a competitive and normative view of school performance. Rather than constituting a reflexive, self-defining process as is suggested in Giddens' (1991) view of institutional reflexivity, school improvement conforms to a technicist change model. It is driven by the standardised knowledge and attainment criteria of the National Curriculum, the rigid regulatory taxonomies of OFSTED inspections, the regimentation and surveillance of various national 'Task Forces', as well as inter-school competition engendered by the publication of national league tables. In the crusade for quality and effectiveness, performance data play an important role in identifying the winners and the losers; separating the 'blue chip' companies (i.e. schools) from those to 'go into liquidation'. Social Darwinism has re-entered the educational frame in that those who can adapt and change to accommodate evolving conditions have a better chance to survive. Yet, ironically, it is not guaranteed that the survivors are necessarily the best educationists.

An essential ingredient in the school effectiveness paradigm is the shift from the social to the organisational context, from the macro to the micro-culture. The White Paper *Excellence in Schools* (DfEE, 1997) supported these meanings. It suggested that:

> *effective change in a field as dependent on human interaction as education requires millions of people to change their behaviour. That will require consistent advocacy and persuasion to create a climate in which schools are constantly challenged to compare themselves to other similar schools and adopt ways of raising their performance* (DfEE, 1997:12, emphasis added).

This surface perspective of change and development highlights the normative view of school performance that underpins contemporary educational policy. Providing no indications of the nature of educational development beyond concerns about measurable 'performativities' and attitudinal changes, this 'benchmarking' reduces educational change to a taken-for-granted shift in perceptions and altering of behaviours. Instead of stimulating local innovation, together, these factors have contributed to organisational isomorphism. According to DiMaggio and Powell (1983, p.150) coercive isomorphism 'results from both formal and informal pressures exerted on organisations by other organisations upon which they are dependent and by cultural expectations within society within which organisations function'. These meanings are reinforced in the Green Paper (1998, p.13) which stresses the importance of 'making the best practice of some schools into the reality for every school'. This view lacks an awareness of the highly differentiated nature of schools and the fact that what constitutes good practice in one school may not necessarily translate to others within different geographic regions, locales and communities. The concept of 'best practice' assumes a predominance of equally distributed functional capabilities. Serving primarily as a rationale for continuous improvement within a circumscribed and regulated framework, it assumes a top-down model of educational change and development.

These meanings draw significantly on Japanese business ideology and production strategies such as the continuous improvement principles of *kaizen* (Morley and Rassool, 1999). Through on-task surveillance and 'neighbourhood checks', workers gain 'best knowledge of work routines', identify problems and in *kaizen* meetings share their 'packages of knowledge' to make suggestions for improvement to the company (Garahan and Stewart, 1992, p.75). However, these industrial meanings do not translate unproblematically to the education context. The focus on comparative levels of institutional performance that inhere in the notion of sharing and adopting cross-school 'best practice' does not overtly, or inherently, address issues related to difference, complexity and inclusion, and peripheralisation. It does not take account of the complexity that class, 'race', gender, sexuality and disability differentials inject into the schooling process. In providing a on homogenised view of schools as neutral production sites in which teachers feature predominantly as functionaries, this micro-contextual approach does not engage *per se* with issues of 'how individuals learn, how knowledge is produced, and how subject positions are constructed' (Giroux, 1992, p.81) within and through the educational system. Nor does it provide the scope to address the relationship between subjective organisational and macro-political societal factors. By focusing only on what is going on *in* schools, and the on-task sensibilities required of teachers, it represents a 'closed system' view of the world (Peters and Waterman, 1995, p.91).

Emphasis on the technicist rationalities of management screen out alternative imaginings and possibilities about what the substantive basis of education can be, or ought to be, within a dynamically changing social world. In teacher education, qualitative shifts have taken place from concerns about pedagogy and learning entitlements towards concerns about the *effectiveness* of schools and the measurement of the *performativity* of teachers. The concept of school *performance* ratified by the Standards Site described in the Green Paper is limited to narrowly defined professional competencies, the regulation of task-oriented institutional practices and processes, systems monitoring and the management of, largely, attitudinal and behavioural change within organisations. In the drive for excellence in schools, specific forms of learning have become exchangeable commodities through which career-paths can be charted in line only with the exigencies of policy. Fast-tracking, and the judicious use of teacher appraisal linked to performance related pay would serve to intensify individual competition amongst teachers and contribute to new inequalities within the profession.

Summary

In a dynamically changing information-based global cultural economy, the reduction of teacher education to the development of linear technical skills and the measurement and regulation of standardised knowledges represents a narrow perspective of social change. The systematised subjectification of teachers, the regulation of ways of knowing and ways of doing, and the social decontextualization of teacher education preclude consideration of social, organisational and educational complexities. The technicist emphasis in the reformulated educational research framework advocated in the Green Paper, reduces the research process to context-specific operational issues. 'Real world' research, within this rigid and closed-systems paradigm, runs the risk of operating within self-referential frames. Serving thus as a centralised regulatory mechanism *par excellence*, it would close off possibilities in teacher education for engagement with broader and critical social knowledges. Already we increasingly find teachers not as cultural workers able to engage freely in critique and self-definition, creating new spaces within which the parameters of educational debate and pedagogical possibility could be redefined. Instead, we find them rigidly locked into the technicism of school effectiveness taxonomies centred on quality control which, in turn, are subjected to a myriad of external and internal bureaucratic forms of control. Theorisations shaped around 'performativity' and work process exclude analysis of societal relations and asymmetries of power within the educational system.

Perhaps most importantly, what is absent from the new professionalism subscribed to in the Green Paper are the affective, ethical awarenesses and the substantive pedagogical knowledges needed to work with pupils. This includes the continuing development of teachers' understanding of teaching and learning processes; their knowledge of culture and the social world. In a dynamically changing social world it is now perhaps more important than ever before that professional development should to extend to an understanding of the multifaceted nature of children's development, and the cognitive, cultural and socio-economic factors that prevent some pupils from full participation in the educational process. This is especially important in a world in which a wide range of social factors such as unemployment, drug addiction, poverty and social dislocation now impact on the everyday experiences of children in schools. Professionalism defined only in procedural and functional managerial terms, would deny teachers an understanding of the diversity that constitutes classrooms and schools. Articulated, as it is, primarily around operational competencies, transmission and measurable standards the new managerial notion of teacher professionalism does not include the negotiation of differential power relations within classrooms between teachers and pupils; between teachers as professionals, and in terms of what is taught, how and why. Embedded in a *mea culpa* sensibility, and a deficit model of development, the new managerial professionalism has a limited perspective of the role of education in the modern world. It makes no allusions to the need to develop discursive ways of engaging with the changing sociocultural learning and informational realities of the global cultural economy.

References

Beck, U. (1992) *Risk Society: Towards a New Modernity,* London: Sage Publications.

DiMaggio, P. and Powell, W. (1983) 'The Iron Cage Revisited: Institutional Isomorphism and Collective Rationality in Organizational Fields'. *American Sociological Review*, 48 (2), 147-160.

De Vroey, M., 1984, A Regulation Approach Interpretation of the Contemporary Crisis, *Capital and Class*, 23, Summer, 45-44.

Department for Education and Employment (DfEE) (1997) *Excellence in Schools*. White Paper presented to Parliament by the Secretary of State for Education and Employment by Command of Her Majesty, July 1997, London: HMSO.

Department for Education and Employment (DfEE) (1998) *Teachers Meeting the Challenge of Change* (Green Paper). London: HMSO.

Garrahan, P. and Stewart, P. (1992) *The Nissan Enigma: Flexibility at Work in a Local Economy*. London: Mansell.

Giddens, A. (1998) *The Third Way: The Renewal of Social Democracy*. London: Polity Press.

Giddens, A. (1991) *Modernity and Self-Identity: Self and Society in the Late Modern Age*, Cambridge: Polity Press.

Giroux, H. (1992) *Border Crossings: Cultural Workers and the Politics of Education,* London: Routledge.

Morley, L. and Rassool, N. (1999) *School Effectiveness: Fracturing the Discourse*. London: Falmer Press.

Peters, T. and Waterson, R. (1995) *In Search of Excellence: Lessons From America's Best-Run Companies,* London: Harper Collins.

Reynolds, D. *et al* (eds.) (1996) *Making Good Schools: Linking School Effectiveness and School Improvement*, London: Routledge.

Slee, R. (1998) 'High Reliability Organizations and Liability Students – The Politics of Recognition', in Slee, R., Weiner, G. and Tomlinson, S. (Eds.), *School Effectiveness for Whom? Challenges to the School Effectiveness and School Improvement Movements*, pp. 101 -114, London: Falmer.

FROM WELFARE TO THE KNOWLEDGE BASED ECONOMY
THE NEW LABOUR OF TEACHING

JIM GRAHAM
UNIVERSITY OF EAST LONDON

We will be accused of being visionary and excessively ambitious. We plead guilty. After the years of drift, vision and ambition are surely what is needed. Creating a world-class education service was never going to be easy but that is what the economy and the society of the future require. A modern profession is central to this process...We urge all those with an interest in the future of our education system ... to grasp the historic opportunity that now presents itself. (Green Paper Teachers: Meeting the Challenge of Change: DfEE 1998a, para. 35)

This chapter argues that economic rationalism is the driving force behind Labour's reform of teaching, and takes precedence over the government's commitments to social justice and to democratic space for local decision making. Ministers have tried to modernise teaching by re-engineering the profession to a post-welfarist specification, and by inserting it into the marketplace for knowledge workers. But this merely highlights the weight of regulatory structures and exposure to public opprobrium which make teaching as a career comparatively unappealing. Arguably, in its obsession with control, the government has seriously misjudged the image which the reformed profession of teaching will present in the job market.

Education, Economy and Social Policy

In the Education White Paper *Excellence in Schools*, David Blunkett outlines New Labour's view of education as strategic investment:

We are talking about investing in human capital in the age of knowledge...to compete in the global economy... (DfEE, 1997a, p3)

Tony Blair has consistently identified economic success as a prerequisite without which all other social policy is financially unattainable. Gordon Brown, in the theatrical *persona* of the Iron Chancellor, has assiduously cultivated his media image of economic rectitude and fiscal prudence. Education is now represented as key plank of economic policy. The performance of the education system is continuously measured against national targets to gauge outcomes produced per tax pound. Employment, or at least assumptions about employability in the near future, shape the skills based curriculum for schools and colleges.

Fundamental to Labour's education policy is the belief that increasingly it will be the production of knowledge, not of manufactured goods, that will constitute the high value added element essential to sustaining a high wage, high skill economy. This vision is laid out in detail in the DTI White Paper *Our Competitive Future: Building the Knowledge Driven Economy* (DTI, 1998). Tony Blair's foreword expresses the government's intention to 'invest where companies alone cannot: in education, science and in the creation of a culture of enterprise' with the intention of exploiting 'our most valuable assets: our knowledge, skills and creativity' which are 'at the heart of a modern knowledge-driven economy'.

Such an *economic rationalist* view of the purposes of education has some obvious and serious limitations (Graham, 1998). Firstly, even if one were to accept the basic primacy of the economic paradigm, the policy justifications emphasise the *supply* side of the equation at the expense of the *demand* side. The vocational function of education in preparing future workers for employability dominates the exchanges between government and employers. What business and industry repeatedly fail to acknowledge is that educated consumers are every bit as important to the economy as educated workers. In the knowledge based economy the education system must also function to create the niched market for cultural products by socialising a population capable of pursuing differentiated demand patterns. The new constituency of consumers is committed to lifestyle choice, supports cultural industries through increasing consumption of media products, and is willing to pay for added-value design features in everyday purchases. This sustains a retail market founded on endless turn-over of fashion items and replacement of obsolescent technology. The characteristics of the educated consumer of a broad spectrum of knowledge-based products are not simply those of the skilled worker producing a subset of those products. So even within its own terms of reference, the vocationalist version of economic rationalism is too one sided to be credible.

Secondly, economic rationalism privileges a particular view of the purposes of education. Some apparently contrary perspectives do exist within Labour's own policies. For example, *Excellence in Schools* repeatedly refers to creating a fairer society, and to broadly based partnerships in public enterprise to rebuild a sense of community. But these apparently altruistic policy goals are easily subsumed later into economic rationality – an unfair society is wasteful of human talent and is therefore inefficient; the financial cost of conflict in the community is a drain on the public purse.

Lastly, objections to economic rationalism derive from philosophical positions which reject utilitarian and materialistic motives in favour of more humanistic values. A learner is more than just a worker or a consumer. Society is more than just a marketplace or an infrastructure for business enterprise. From this stance, education is arguably worthwhile for its own sake; it may be seen as a public good and as an individual human right in civil society; each learner is entitled to self-actualisation; education is a necessity for participation in democracy; and education is essential for a sustainable future on the planet.

Global economic change

The changes to society and economy which underpin New Labour's embrace of the market in the 'Third Way' (Giddens, 1998) are attributed to global economic phenomena sometimes described as the shift from *Fordism* to *post-Fordism*[1]. Fordism refers the mass production of standardised goods for a mass market, characterised by industrialisation up to and including the post-war period. But in recent years mass production has saturated the market for basic consumer goods in the economies of the western world. To maintain consumption – and therefore production – consumer *needs* for mass standardised goods are replaced by the stimulation of *wants* driven more by desire, fashion, image and perceived obsolescence, than by basic function of the product itself. In consequence the west has de-industrialised by exporting heavy industry and its pollution problems to low wage/low skill economies in the developing world. Western economic policy now tries to monopolise information-intensive and new technology-intensive processes in added value flexible production requiring skilled knowledge workers.

The term *post-Fordism* thus refers to a gradual transition to a post-industrial economy in which more flexible modes of production and distribution create profit through by increasing the knowledge component of goods. Examples of these value-added knowledge elements include design of clothing or cars, or cultural commodities like films and computer software. The theory suggests that to sustain this production and consumption, the population needs to be highly educated and skilled, and must be flexible enough through continuous retraining to keep pace with the fast-moving knowledge market.[2] Under post-Fordism, government management of the infrastructure for production shifts from supporting heavy industry through the regulation of such matters as transport, energy, and the importation of raw materials from the (ex)colonies, to creating the conditions for the knowledge-based economy to flourish. In order to deal with these new forms of production, the state has to reinvent its modes of control, and this may involve politicians in abandoning cherished discourses which have served to justify previous configurations. New Labour's careful distancing from old socialist policies such as nationalisation is a case in point.

Thus the White Paper *Our Competitive Future* (DTI, 1998) redefines Labour's view about the relationship between the state and the market. The challenge, writes Blair, is 'to create and execute a new approach to industrial policy' because 'old fashioned state intervention did not and cannot work. But neither does naïve reliance on markets'. National policies, it suggests, cannot buck European and global market pressures. The paper goes on to herald 'a new model for public policy' (DTI, 1998, ch.1) which rejects the interventionist planning of the isolated nation state espoused by previous Labour governments. The preferred alternative is the state's management of the infrastructure for competitiveness – including the modernisation of markets – coupled to strategic investment in the skills base against defined targets. The goal is a 'flexible, innovative and entrepreneurial economy' with minimum regulation.

But some areas of the market are deemed to require more intervention than others, and the education system is a case in point. Schools are presented as so fundamental to the development of the human capital on which the prosperity of the economy is based, that the state must regulate rigorously to guarantee the performance of the system. This is coded as 'achieving a world class education service' by the government's adviser, Michael Barber (1998). David Blunkett writes that, 'like you, we want world-class schools in the new century. In a world of rapid change...' (DfEE, 1998a, foreword). The body of the Green Paper reiterates this mantra:

Creating a world-class education service was never going to be easy but that is what the economy and the society of the future require. A modern profession is central to this process... (DfEE, 1998a para. 35)

The conventional wisdom set out in *Excellence in Schools* blames national economic failure on under-performing schools and this is the fault of an inadequately skilled and poorly managed teaching profession. On the basis of this deficit view of the system, and a pathological view of teachers, the discourse of economic rationalism legitimates direct intervention in the processes of schooling and the control of teachers' work. Teaching must be 'modernised', that is, brought within a system of more stringent managerialist control. The outcome is a panoply of regulation in the name of raising standards, including a revised National Curriculum and a unified qualifications framework (QCA), prescribed methods for teaching basic skills (Standards and Effectiveness Unit's National Literacy and Numeracy Strategies) and mandatory occupational standards imposed on the teaching profession by TTA.

The Green Paper restructures line management, pay and promotion into a 'New Deal' for teachers which is designed to reform teachers' work and performance. Will this halt the drift away from teaching by well qualified applicants, and restore the flagging morale of the profession? Arguably, the most serious threats to 'raising standards' and to the achievement of a 'world class education service' are the low status of the profession, and the inability to recruit teachers for key curriculum subject like science, Information Technology and maths. Do the proposals make the profession attractive in the new marketplace competition for knowledge workers?

Beyond Welfarism

Workers are, as du Gay (1996, p55) remarks, 'discursively re-imagined and conceptualised at different times through their repositioning in a variety of discourses of work reform'. Government policy has shifted the discourse about teacher professionalism from that of welfare workers in the post-war era, to that of knowledge professionals in today's global market.

Following the economic crises of the 1970s and the Callaghan government's initial forays into intervention, accountability and cut-backs in the public services, the subsequent New Right governments in the 1980s and early 1990s set about dismantling the post-war welfarist settlement. This had been based on a democratic consensus about social policies which guaranteed standardised care through nationalised industries providing health, education and social services. These mass welfare services were the equivalent of the mass consumer goods of Fordist production. They represented every citizen's right to a social wage, available (at least in theory) equally to all. The New Right replaced the welfarist consensus with a commitment to possessive individualism and free market ideology that entailed rolling back the 'nanny state' and opening up market forces in established areas of state benefits such as education, health, housing, employment and pensions. New Labour's 'Third Way' (Giddens, 1998) has continued these reforms.

For the cadre of state professionals whose numbers burgeoned in the post-war period, such market reforms have conflicted with the public service ethic. Teaching, for example, was represented as a vocation in which the personal reward of high pay was discounted for altruistic reasons. The professional gift relationship underpinned interactions with pupils. Job satisfaction came from public esteem for the task of contributing to the common wealth and to society's future. But what Gewirtz (1997) termed the post-welfarist education complex of interdependent policies of educational reform, has turned schools into mini-businesses, imposed central control on the curriculum, and required professional accountability for performance against targets. Teachers became embroiled in the contradictions of a state controlled quasi-market, neither free to follow the risks and rewards of the commercial market, nor secure in the public sector welfarist ethos. Gewirtz argues that *teachers are experiencing a loss of autonomy and an accelerated intensification of activity and stress; there is a decline in the sociability of teaching; and there is pressure on teachers to adopt more traditional pedagogies, with a focus on output rather than process, and on particular groups of higher attaining students.* (Gewirtz, 1997, p.230)

Demoralisation and falling recruitment have resulted as 'failing' schools and 'incompetent' teachers have been publicly named, blamed and shamed by politicians from successive governments in search of a soft target and an easy sound-bite. The present crisis in teacher supply which has precipitated this urgent action over teachers' salary levels is arguably a direct consequence of these policies.

The Green Paper and Performance Management

The government's presumption seems to be that, given effective leadership and stringent performance management of staff, schools can compensate for social and environmental factors. In his review of school improvement research to date, Mortimore (1998) suggests that such measures can have only a limited impact. Drawing on his work with Whitty (Mortimore and Whitty, 1997) he maintains his view that school factors can make a difference, but acknowledges that social class differences in cultural capital are prime determinants of a school's absolute level of success. The situation is exacerbated by the polarising effect of parental choice in the marketplace, as socially and geographically mobile families converge on 'star' schools and abandon 'sink' schools to the poor and powerless.

Can the method for the determination of teachers' pay raise educational attainment? The government appears to believe that the present salary structure lacks sufficient incentives and controls. As elsewhere in the public sector, the solution is to change the balance of pressure and support to couple pay more directly to outputs. The Green Paper proposes to stratify the teaching profession further by introducing new performance related pay based on annual appraisal, linking access to the higher grades in the profession to proven achievement in raising standards by implementing approved pedagogies. Headteacher's pay will be determined by governors on the basis of the attainment of school improvement targets such as gains in pupil performance. In turn, headteachers will appraise and reward staff down the hierarchy on the evidence of their professional contribution to raising standards. The widespread introduction of teaching assistants and teaching associates creates a sub-teacher grade, so that in future classroom teachers will manage the work of other adults. While this eases some of the problems of the shortage of qualified teachers, it also locks classroom teachers into a position of responsibility for others in the performance management cycle.

The entire enterprise works on the management by objectives model (MBO). The curriculum is centrally planned and prescribed. Local quality and performance data are derived from standardised tests and inspection reports. As 'managing director' of the local educational enterprise, the headteacher sets out the vision of the school. The School Development Plan establishes the action plan and sets new targets which are translated into personal objectives by the annual appraisal process for all staff. Differential remuneration is the carrot and stick to ensure compliance.

A number of problems are apparent with this whole approach. MBO is based on Taylorist work study (Morgan, 1986; Graham, 1997a). It assumes that it is possible to select the right performance variables, and to measure these accurately in order to determine the objectives in the first place. This may work in routine production engineering using machines, but is arguably ill-suited to complex human interactions and problem solving. In effect, MBO may reduce the complexity of schooling to a few performance indicators to be pursued at all costs by rational staff in the rational organisation, regardless of the collateral damage. Similar problems have arisen elsewhere, when QANGOs have pursued the logic of their own narrow remits regardless of the impact on other areas of social policy – for example, the Child Support Agency financially destabilising second families, or Health Trusts implementing cost saving on their own budgets by abandoning patients to tokenistic Care in the Community. The tunnel vision caused by limited objectives and constrained definitions of local and immediate efficiency and effectiveness may not be in the longer term interests of pupils, parents or schools – or of the economy.

In specifying the characteristics of a world class education service, Barber (1998) cites 'extensive autonomy at school level' as the number one factor, and goes on to refer to a 'highly developed capacity to manage change' and to 'prepare for the future through encouraging controlled and targeted experimentation'. However, the Green Paper proposals may actually be one more turn of the screw in generating a culture of compliance in schools, in which all important educational decisions about the content and pace of the curriculum and the nature of the pupils' educational experiences are mandated by central agencies – QCA curricula, OFSTED school inspections, prescriptions from the Standards and Effectiveness unit, and targets to improve SAT performance.

'The role of teachers facing the challenges of rapid social and educational change' was the topic of an OECD paper based on the work from the Centre for Educational Research and Innovation (CERI) discussed at the 1996 UNESCO 45th International Conference on Education. The authors identified *school malaise syndrome* as a problem which was prevalent world-wide, caused by bureaucratic intervention and over-centralisation of control of education systems. They concluded that,

> *The more complex a professional activity becomes, the more policy interventions have to take into account the views of practitioners and leave space for local adaptations. This assumption is based on the understanding that in complex modern societies many local practical problems cannot be solved for the institutions by central regulations. Instead, the problem solving capacity of these institutions and of the persons working in them has to be improved... Innovations in complex situations cannot be cloned... The principle implies that any sub-stantial innovation must be 'acquired' by teachers in a very personal sense. This means that they must be able to transform it...* (OECD, 1996, p11)

The OECD authors advocate more collegial and collaborative modes of control, and less bureaucratic prescription. The key question is whether or not the Green Paper's proposals for performance management will enable teachers to become transformative professionals working in partnership with local communities, or whether the compliance culture will simply be reinforced. The precedents in the past two decades of steadily increasing state regulation are not encouraging. Neither is there any evidence to suggest that the politician's distrust of producer capture by educationalists has relaxed – indeed, at a recent debate on the Green Paper in London[3],

Blunkett criticised teacher collegiality as a vehicle for complacency about the lowest common denominator in school performance.

Mortimore (1999) maintains that the Green Paper's proposed performance management scheme is the wrong answer to the wrong question. He suggests that better value would be achieved for the same the money if it was targeted on eliminating the present disparities in school resourcing, and on attempting to compensate for the inequalities in cultural capital which the most disadvantaged children suffer. Spending money on performance related pay for individual staff is likely to have a negative impact because it undermines the necessary collaborative structure of teaching for school improvement.

The African proverb that 'It takes a whole village to raise a child' applies equally to schools. Arguably it takes a whole school to educate a child, and all teachers plus parents and community partners contribute their expertise. In a cumulative and developmental process, where effects are often delayed over years, it is almost impossible to attribute a child's learning to a single intervention. The time scales of change are not the same as industrial production line engineering, where recalibration of the welding robots to tighter tolerances brings immediate measurable quality outcomes. Influences in education are often indirect, as maturation or emotional factors come gradually into play. In assuming rapid payoff from teaching to produce observed outcomes, the government's underlying pedagogical prejudices about transmissive teaching and direct instruction are plainly visible.

Personal performance related pay for teachers constitutes the individualisation of institutional problems – or even of wider social problems – by locating the blame in particular professionals, whose salary is adjusted commensurately. Given the structural problems of social exclusion and their influence on school performance, this is likely to demotivate those who work in the most difficult schools with the hardest children to teach.

The conclusion is that better results in raising standards, improving schools and motivating teachers are likely to be achieved by improving teachers' autonomy, not by diminishing it. The high accountability, low trust culture reinforced by a mechanistic and hierarchical approach to the control of the profession contrasts markedly with initiatives elsewhere. For example, the Norwegian school system is pursuing improvement through peer evaluation and collegiality, deliberately avoiding the pitfalls of bureaucratic centralism to ensure democratic ownership of change by school, communities and professionals (Granheim, 1997). The Green Paper is a further manifestation of the government's 'control freak' tendencies, and may well backfire by further alienating prospective recruits to the profession.

Enterprising Knowledge Professionals for the 21st century?

The DTI White Paper Our *Competitive Future: Building the Knowledge Based Economy* (DTI, 1998) refers throughout to the need to promote creativity, flexibility, enterprise and risk-taking as essential ingredients of a flourishing knowledge industry. Tony Blair's emphasis on these aspects in the foreword to the DTI White Paper contrasts oddly with the dirigiste obsessions which permeate the Green Paper for teachers. If the former are indeed to be the defining characteristics of knowledge professionals in the next century, how many high flying graduates will choose a teaching career that promises uncertain pay, constant criticism in the media and perpetual close scrutiny of individual performance?

The surveillance regime is already exhaustive. Intending teachers must satisfy the rigorous entry selection criteria in Circular 4/98 (DfEE, 1998b) specifying curriculum expertise and personal qualities. Postgraduates must possess GCSE English, Maths and Science as well as a relevant degree. Under Green Paper proposals, regardless of this they will be subjected to further entry tests in English, Maths and Information Technology. Once on the Initial Teacher Training (ITT) course, primary students for example will be required to develop upwards of 2000 assessable attributes set out as standards descriptors in Circular 4/98. These must be audited at final assessment, and new TTA appointed external examiners will verify the achievements. Students leave ITT with a Career Entry Profile, to be interviewed for a teaching post as a Newly Qualified Teacher. Appointment leads into compulsory induction with a further round of assessment against the standards for Qualified Teacher Status. Once confirmed in post, annual performance appraisal includes observation of teaching and monitoring of pupil performance. Progression beyond the performance threshold on the salary scale depends on good results. Promotion to

Advanced Skills Teacher, or further to headteacher, entails assessment and verification of compliance with more sets of occupational standards. Schools are inspected by OFSTED every four years, and the performance of each teacher is a matter for report. New technology prompts the collection and analysis of detailed pupil performance data. The school has an annual Development Plan, and each teacher's appraisal is linked to it. Teachers meet parents regularly, and governors make an annual report to parents. OFSTED and SATs outcomes, at school, LEA and national levels are published as league tables and each focusses the agenda for political comment which is frequently adverse, ill-informed and demotivating.

While most professions involve public accountability in one form or another, few can be subjected to such unremitting surveillance: teachers suffer assessment, testing, examination, audit, appraisal, inspection, review and reporting, leading inevitably to frequent public criticism. Teaching as a career, in its post-welfarist incarnation, has to compete with the catalogue of other knowledge professions trying to attract recruits. Other professions may well offer greater scope for autonomy, creativity and public esteem. In a post-modern society, choosing a career means choosing a future identity, adopting a consciousness and a value system, stylising and constructing both the self image and the presented self (Graham, 1997b). In these terms, teaching has little attraction as an aspirational identity.

Moving teaching squarely into the global marketplace means that global market rules apply for the supply and demand for skilled workers. The irony is that the recruitment campaigns currently run by the TTA attempt to capitalise on the old public service ethic, emphasising the job satis-factions in working with young people, with the slogan that 'No one forgets a good teacher'. This advertising exploits the very images and mythology of teacher professionalism from a different era which the Green Paper so systematically dismantles. Perhaps TTA believes that hard information about the control structures and salary levels in the profession make poor copy.

The government asserts that the Green Paper represents an 'historic oppor-tunity' to be 'visionary and excessively ambitious' (DfEE, 1998a para. 35), but the pompous rhetoric is as facile as the reforms are unimaginative and bureaucratically rigid. The much-vaunted New Deal for teachers may turn out to be a Bad Deal. It is difficult to see ambitious graduates opting for teaching in the new dispensation proposed by the Green Paper. Graduates might just as well – and probably will – join other professions which offer more creative space, better rewards and less stress. If teachers really are to be the lynchpin knowledge professionals on whom the economic prosperity of Britain in the C21st depends, we must have serious reservations about the viability and attractiveness of the government's proposals. Unless many more young people see teaching as the career of choice, New Labour's protestations about creating a world class education service will founder on the rock of teacher shortage. Even by its own narrow and simplistic economic rationalist criteria, the government will fail to deliver its promises to the electorate.

References

Barber, M. (1998) 'Creating a World Class Education Service', paper to North of England Conference, Bradford, 5-7 January 1998.

Brown, P. and Lauder, H. (1996) 'Education, Globalization and Economic Development' *J. Education Policy*, vol.11, no. 1, pp1-25.

DfEE (1997a) *Excellence in Schools* White Paper Cm3681 Stationery Office July 1997.

DfEE (1998a) *Teachers: Meeting the Challenge of Change Green Paper*, Cm 4164, London: The Stationery Office, December 1998.

DfEE (1998b) Circular 4/98 *Teaching: High Status, High Status, High Standards*, London: DfEE.

DTI (1998) *Our Competitive Future: Building the Knowledge Driven Economy* White Paper December.

duGay, P. (1996) *Consumption and Identity at Work* London: Sage.

Gewirtz, S., (1997) 'Post-welfarism and the Reconstruction of Teachers' Work' *J. Education Policy* vol.12, no.4, pp. 217-231.

Giddens, A. (1998) *The Third Way: the Renewal of Social Democracy* London: Polity.

Graham J. (1997a) 'The National Curriculum for Teacher Training – Playing Politics or Promoting Professionalism?' *British Journal of Inservice Education*, vol. 23, no. 2, pp 163-177.

Graham J. (1997b) 'Postmodernism, Post-Fordism and Consumerism: Marketising Mass Higher Education' in DaCosta, C. and Gokulsing, K. (eds) (1997) *Usable Knowledges as the Goal of University Education*, New York: Mellen Press, pp119-152.

Graham J. (1998) 'From New Right to New Deal: Nationalism, Globalisation and the Regulation of Teacher Professionalism', *Journal of Inservice Education*, vol. 24, no. 1, pp. 9-29.

Granheim, M., (1997) 'Evaluating the School System: A Norwegian Perspective' Keynote speech given at the North of England Education Conference, Sheffield, January 4, 1997.

Morgan, G. (1986) *Images of Organisation* London: Sage.

Mortimore P., and Whitty G., (1997) *Can School Improvement Overcome the Effects of Disadvantage?* Institute of Education, London.

Mortimore P. (1998) *The Road to School Improvement: reflections on school effectiveness* Lisse: Swets and Zeitlinger.

Mortimore, P. (1999) 'The Voice of Concern', *Guardian Education* 15 January 199, p3.

OECD (1996) 'An overview of OECD work on teachers, their pay and conditions, teaching quality and the continuing professional development of teachers': paper to the 45th International Conference on Education, UNESCO, Geneva 30 Sept. – 5 Oct. 1996.

Notes

1 This remains a contested concept, which refers to uneven trends and debatable determinants – see Kumar (1995).

2 The alternative is the flexible economy based on low skill and low wage, sometimes referred to as neo-Fordism (Brown and Lauder, 1996) .

3 Reply to questions at the *Guardian Education* Debate, Institute of Education, London, 26 January 1999.

INDEX